The Lifelong Learning Sector
Reflective Reader

The Lifelong Learning Sector Reflective Reader

Edited by
Susan Wallace

LearningMatters

First published in 2010 by Learning Matters Ltd

British Library Cataloguing in Publication Data
A CIP record for this book is available from the British Library.

ISBN 978 1 84445 296 5

Cover design by Topics – The Creative Partnership
Text design by Code 5
Project management by Deer Park Productions, Tavistock, Devon
Typeset by PDQ Typesetting Ltd, Staffordshire
Printed and bound in Great Britain by Bell & Bain Ltd, Glasgow

Learning Matters Ltd
33 Southernhay East
Exeter EX1 1NX
Tel: 01392 215560
Email: info@learningmatters.co.uk
www.learningmatters.co.uk

Mixed Sources
Product group from well-managed
forests and other controlled sources
www.fsc.org   Cert no. TT-COC-002769
© 1996 Forest Stewardship Council

FSC

Contents

Introduction

The current drive to establish teaching as a postgraduate level profession applies to colleges in the Lifelong Learning sector (LLS) just as it does to schools. To support the current requirement for a scholarly dimension to their teacher training or continuing professional development (CPD), this book provides teachers, tutors and student teachers in the sector with a selection of chapters on topics and issues of immediate relevance to them, combining the format of academic papers with an accessible style and clear, relevant, sector-specific content. It aims to both engage and challenge the reader. It is designed not only for trainee teachers but also for all those teachers in the sector who wish to gain the best possible experience from their CPD. As well as addressing key issues, its purpose is also to cover the required theory-related knowledge content of the professional standards. It is designed as an essential resource to support the requirement set out in the Lifelong Learning UK (LLUK) professional standards that teachers should engage with scholarship, particularly in their specialist subject area. 'Engaging with scholarship' means, among other things, that teachers need to know where to look for sources of information, ideas and debate; how to navigate, read and summarise professional and academic publications effectively; and how to present their own arguments and disseminate their own best practice in the form of reports, assignments and research papers. To build the confidence of teachers and student teachers in these skills, this book sets out to provide a 'bridge' between professional development texts for the sector, which necessarily focus largely on practice, and those scholarly, theoretical, academic texts found in academic and professional journals which, to many, may be unfamiliar territory. Its primary aim, therefore, is to provide busy practitioners and student teachers with an introduction to scholarly analysis and academic writing *which is relevant to their current qualifications, their working lives and their professional development.*

The nature of the LLS means that many of its teachers are drawn from industry, commerce and trades, and enter the teaching profession with significant and valuable expertise in their vocational area. Often this means that their successful pre-teaching career has not involved an engagement with formal, scholarly texts. Moreover, teacher training and CPD for the LLS now include the option, and in some places the requirement, for study at Masters level. Masters level requires a knowledge of relevant literature and an ability to engage critically with it. It is currently difficult for tutors to find relevant texts which *effectively support teachers and student teachers in this sector in taking that step* from a professional graduate to a postgraduate level of study. This book is designed to meet that need.

Common themes run through several of these chapters. Not surprisingly, the most frequently encountered theme is that of *change,* and the recent rapid developments in policy, legislation and qualifications which are continuing to shape the sector. Another is that of *reflective practice* and its centrality to the development of professional skills. *Inclusion* is also a dominant theme, which appears in several of the chapters; as is *professionalism* and the application of the LLUK professional standards for teachers. The recurrence of these themes in chapters with quite disparate topics provides the reader with an opportunity to consider each of them from a variety of viewpoints and in a number of different contexts. The reader is also able to see how differently writers may muster an effective argument and assemble their evidence, even when discussing the same issue. In this way the book does not present just one uniform template for academic writing, but shows that, within the common conventions and principles, different approaches in terms of voice, structure, content and style are both possible and acceptable.

This is well illustrated by the different levels of accessibility represented by the writing collected here, which ranges from the straightforward and simply expressed – such as we might find in a professional publication – to the more complex and densely argued writing of the kind found in some academic journals. It is now an expectation of teachers in the sector that they should engage with both these types of publication, both to support the development of their teaching skills and to reinforce and update their subject knowledge. The range offered here, therefore, provides an ideal opportunity for the reader who wishes to build up confidence by starting with, for example, Chapters 1, 2, 5 and 8 – where the language and structure are less complex – and then moving on to the more demanding models of academic writing to be found in, say, Chapters 4, 7 and 10.

In this way, each chapter serves its double purpose by addressing a topic or issue of immediate relevance to teachers and student teachers in the sector while at the same time presenting a model of good practice in academic writing. A short preface to each chapter points out particular features which the reader should look out for (for example, the correct conventions for the setting out and referencing of quotes). Each chapter closes with a set of suggested tasks and discussion points, which are designed to encourage readers to engage closely with the chapter's content, to explore its relevance to their own practice, and to develop their skills and confidence in exploring the related academic and professional literature relevant to their own teaching.

Since part of its purpose is to serve as a template for scholarly writing, the main body of each chapter includes an abstract, a brief profile of the author and a list of references to texts cited. And because this is a collection of chapters written by different authors, the book presents arguments and theories on key topics through a number of different voices and viewpoints, including those of managers and mentors as well as those of trainers and teachers. In this way, as well as demonstrating how arguments can be constructed from different points of view, it recognises the urgent need to provide a contextual overview of the sector for those who are new to the profession.

The chapters are sequenced in such a way as to reflect teachers' unfolding experiences of the sector from initial training and their entry into teaching, through the processes of developing good practices in supporting learning, to a wider understanding of contextual and whole-college issues such as the application of national policy and the importance of CPD.

The first three chapters deal with the individual teacher, definitions of the teacher's role within the sector and matters relating to the planning of learning. Chapter 1 considers how previous experience can shape our teaching. It introduces the concept of preferred 'teaching styles' and how these often arise from our own previous experiences of education. It explores how we might extend our range of teaching styles, moving out of our comfort zone, and why this might be desirable. It also questions whether there is a significant connection between 'teaching style' and 'learning style'. It is followed by discussion and guidance on style and tone, and on the use of the first person, 'I' in academic writing. Chapter 2 then provides both an overview and a critical analysis of the background to the introduction of the professional standards. It gently introduces the concept of discourse analysis, and provides in itself a clear template for this sort of analytical writing. As a useful summary of the policies that have recently reshaped further education (FE) it will be particularly helpful to trainee teachers unfamiliar with the sector. The tasks that follow it provide the reader with guidance on key aspects of formal academic writing, including abbreviations, acronyms and abstracts. Chapter 3 goes on to explore the function of the lesson plan and looks at some research into how such plans are viewed and used (or not used) by teachers in the sector. It provides a model or template of how an enquiry such as this can be written up formally as a research paper. The tasks that follow explain some of the conventions and presentational issues which are important for teachers to be aware of when reading or writing research papers.

The following three chapters address key issues relating to inclusive practice. Chapter 4 examines the idea of the FE college as a 'second chance' route for learners who have not fulfilled their potential through the traditional route of secondary schooling, or who choose to resume their education and training as adults. It looks at current theories of 'second chance' and adult learning and analyses the implications for approaches to teaching. Its tasks provide guidance on how to cite relevant literature correctly and how quotation and citation can be used effectively in academic writing to support an argument. Chapter 5 examines current theories about the teaching and supporting of functional skills in the sector. It invites readers to compare their own experiences and observations to the theories cited. The tasks that follow it focus on the use of chronologies, reference material, and personal experience, and how best these can be presented to support and illustrate academic argument. Chapter 6 draws on current theory and research to consider questions both about how assessment is used (and sometimes over-used) in teaching, and whether current assessment practices, for example in subjects such as information and communication technology (ICT), are fit for purpose. It is followed by tasks which explore the conventions governing the use of appendices in formal writing.

The final four chapters return to the teacher's role, this time as a member of the team and the institution within which they practise. These chapters present the teacher in the context of their career trajectory and CPD. Chapter 7 explores the theory and uses of reflective practice, incorporating an introduction to action research. This chapter looks at ways in which reflective and reflexive practices enhance professionalism and contribute to developmental action planning. Its tasks provide guidance on the use of section headings and topic sentences. Chapter 8 looks at questions of belonging and collegiality and explores the idea of the learning organisation and communities of practice. It provides an introduction to current theories and focuses on the role of the teacher as subject specialist, examining ways in which diverse subjects and vocational areas interact and co-exist within FE colleges, and the way in which status or esteem is attributed. The tasks look at referencing works by more than one author, and referencing websites. Following on this theme of the subject specialist, Chapter 9 explores current theories relating to mentoring, and looks at ways in which such theories can be applied and tested in an LLS context. It raises the question of how individuals' experience of being mentored can vary widely – an issue which is particularly relevant to the sector and is a recurring theme in OFSTED reports on teacher training. The tasks that follow encourage the reader to engage with specialised vocabulary relevant to their role as educators; and with the synthesis of information – a skill necessary not only for academic writing but also essential for teaching and supporting learning. Chapter 10 takes the institution itself as its focus. It examines the way in which external and internal factors – such as government policy and the CPD needs of teachers – shape college practices and policies. It provides an opportunity for readers to consider some of the management issues and wider contexts which underpin their own work, and introduces them to theoretical models. The tasks that follow this chapter provide guidance on the use of charts and graphs; useful phrases for introducing quotes; how to reference quotes from newspapers; how to use the term 'ibid'; and how the use of figurative language can enliven a piece of writing.

Two Appendices are provided at the end of this book. One sets out the areas of the professional standards covered by each chapter; the other provides an alphabetical index of the professional skills for reading and writing, and the chapters in which they can be found. A chapter by chapter list is also provided.

It is hoped that this collection of chapters on topics and issues of immediate relevance to teachers and student-teachers in the LLS will support teachers in meeting the current requirement for a scholarly dimension to their teacher training or CPD, and will provide a bridge to further study for aspiring members of what we are promised will be 'a postgraduate level profession'.

1
How previous experience can shape our teaching

The aims of this chapter are to provide:

- a discussion of the place of learning styles and teaching styles;
- examination of the teacher's experiences and how they influence their initial teaching style;
- an overview of how the issue of learning styles influences a teacher's approach;
- thought-provoking discussion around the notion of the 'comfort zone' in a teacher's practice.

What to look for

- Note the style and tone of this paper, including the use of the first person, 'I', and the way the author refers to his own professional experience.
- Use the suggested steps provided to help you to audit your own teaching style and preferences.

Author details

Neil Stott is currently a lecturer in education studies at Nottingham Trent University where he is the Programme Leader for In-Service Professional Graduate/Certificate in Education (LLS). He worked in FE for 22 years as an engineering tutor, teaching craft and technician levels including Computer Aided Design and Quality Assurance. Having a professional and personal interest in curriculum development, he became responsible for the development of various courses outside of engineering and was latterly a Curriculum Area Leader for Management, Education and Training – with particular responsibility for In-Service and Pre-Service Lifelong Learning Sector (LLS) Teacher Education.

How previous experience can shape our teaching

Neil Stott

Abstract

This chapter introduces the concept of preferred 'teaching styles' and how these often arise from our own previous experiences of education. It explores how we might extend our range of teaching styles, moving ourselves out of our comfort zone; and why this might be desirable. It also questions whether there is a significant connection between 'teaching style' and 'learning style'.

Introduction

Over the last two decades there have been many changes in the adult learning curriculum within the LLS. One has only to track, for example, how the sector has been variously described during that time – *Further Education, Post Compulsory Education and Training* and, most recently, *Lifelong Learning* – to see how external forces have sought to change perception and emphasis. Yet at the core of this diversity lies a conundrum: What exactly *is* an LLS teacher and how should one teach?

Teaching in LLS is a very diverse profession and LLS lecturers may teach in any of the following settings: general or specialist FE colleges, tertiary colleges, sixth form colleges, HM Prisons, armed forces education centres, company training centres, and diverse private training organisations (DfES, 2004).

Consider, by way of a case study, a certain engineering craftsman who worked hard in industry and was in possession of a full technical certificate, gained over a decade. This craftsman worked independently and also had an important yet informal role in the training and care of apprentices. This was an unrecognised and under-valued role yet it was tradi-tional, accepted and formative for the trainee. There was no formal training involved for this position; it was often down to an intuitive judgement by a junior manager and, to some extent, a question of the luck of the draw when decisions were made over 'who trained who'.

This unstructured and somewhat arcane method of training for apprentices ran alongside formal off-the-job training followed by 'day release' at a local technical college or 'tech', with little connection or communication between employers, on the job trainers and, most impor-tantly for this chapter, those teaching the apprentices one day a week in college.

Let's 'fast forward' then to the scenario of that same engineer, now recruited to a college where he will be teaching within his own vocational area. How did he start, what did he do and how successfully did he do it in this first phase of his career? Perhaps almost inevitably there was a tendency to default to the way he himself had been taught. This was in a largely didactic way, with the linear and constrained syllabus being somewhat unimaginatively interpreted. We shall leave him there for now and see how he progresses.

Since our fictional engineer began his teaching career, the LLS curriculum has changed considerably, reflecting the subsequent decline of manufacturing and other traditional industries and sectors. However, the staffing needs of colleges and other LLS employers mean that they still need to recruit experienced individuals from thriving vocational areas to take on an effective teaching and learning role. While a sizeable minority do enter the LLS teaching profession after following a full-time Postgraduate Certificate in Education (PGCE), Professional Graduate Certificate in Education (Prof GCE) or Certificate in Education course, the main entrants are still 'career-changers' drawn through similar routes taken by our fictional engineer; and this is still widely held to be a career advance-ment for those individuals. In other words, the LLS still needs to convert vocational experts to teachers; and this cannot be done effectively without due consideration for the changes of attitudes, motivations and skills required in transforming the professional identity of these skilled individuals from practitioner to teacher in a relatively short space of time. Moreover, given the period of change and the instrumentalist nature of the LLS, the new reality means that teachers within it are, more than ever, obliged to take into consideration the attendant demands of increased learner expectation, institutional requirements and pressure on institutions to raise 'success rates' within the Quality Assurance (QA) standards laid down by the external agencies involved with the funding and governance of the sector.

Learning style and teaching styles

Following the recent changes within the standards for the training of teachers in LLS, teachers are now more than ever encouraged to consider students' individual preferences for, and responses to, different ways of learning. Indeed, much is made of 'learning styles' in general and particularly the model based on Kolb's (1984) work, which has been developed by Honey and Mumford (1992). This has been used widely – if not always wisely – in FE colleges and across education and training; and there is much debate and discussion around this aspect of initial assessment of learners. Coffield et al (2004) conducted wide-ranging research into the pedagogical implications of the use – and misuse – of learning styles across the sector and their study indicates the controversy surrounding their deployment. Indeed they suggest that:

> For some, learning styles have become an unquestioned minor part of their professional thinking and practice, which allows them to differentiate students quickly and simply; for others, the same instruments are considered both unreliable and invalid and so they do not use them in practice.

> (Ibid, p44)

This suggests that teachers should investigate the efficacy of learning style surveys with a critical eye before making pedagogical decisions based on their use. Far less attention, however, is given to what we shall term 'preferred *teaching* style'. In practice, information about their students' learning styles is most useful to teachers when considered side by side with an honest and open appraisal of the teacher's own preferred style of teaching.

Remember that engineering teacher in our case study? He did not have any idea about learning styles or teaching styles. He formed his own idea of how to teach based on his own experience of being taught, and on his experience of being a workplace trainer. This meant that much of his early development as an FE teacher was through trial and error. As a consequence, his initial transformation into a teacher was a difficult one and his learners were, perhaps, poorly served as a result.

What exactly *is* a teaching style?

Naturally, individual teaching styles reflect diverse elements driven by the psychological make-up of teachers, their formative experiences both as vocational and/or academic practitioners and, often importantly, their attitude to their learners. Indeed, a definition of teaching style could well be implicit in the relationship that exists between teachers and their learners – the feasible options for teaching and learning activity that are available in the complex interactions between the teacher's behaviour and that of the learners.

Mosston and Ashworth (1990) contend that teachers should not rely on a single style but should consider options based on observed styles of learning (beyond simple screening and categorisation of students) and design structures based on decisions made during dialogue with learners. They suggest that the spectrum of styles differs in terms of both teaching and learning behaviour and that they range (11 in all) from control by the teacher – *command style* – to learner autonomy within a style which Mosston and Ashworth define as *self teaching*.

As most FE colleges currently include higher education (HE) study within their curriculum, there is now potential for learners to progress from modest levels of study within the National Qualification Framework (NQF) up to entry level HE, such as Higher National Certificates/Diplomas and Foundation Degrees – and even franchised first degree courses. More importantly, for the theme of this paper, it also means that many FE teachers may find themselves teaching HE level courses. Biggs (1999), writing principally for the university teaching sector, identifies a four-level process where students construct meaning from what they do to learn. The teacher constructively aligns planned learning activity and assessment with the learning outcomes. Biggs suggests that learners should be encouraged to take more responsibility for learning as they develop – and this has huge implications for the practice and style of teachers in post-compulsory education. Considered alongside Grasha's (1996) typology of teaching styles – Expert, Formal Authority, Personal Model, Facilitator and Delegator – the converging trend is towards more learner autonomy the further the individual progresses to higher levels of education and training, or the higher their own ability level rises. Clearly this has important implications for the styles of teaching necessary to support learning as it progresses.

Direct teaching style

Often referred to as *instructional* or *direct instructional* style, this is a way of teaching that relies almost entirely on the teacher being the expert in the topic and sole arbiter (within the constraints of the syllabus or programme specification) of *what should be learned* at the time of the instruction. Direct teaching styles have an important place in the area of teaching skills but may be less appropriate for learning at higher cognitive levels or in the affective domain.

Of course this does not mean to say that direct teaching is in some way a *lesser* technique compared to others, but simply that it can be misused or misplaced – perhaps by default.

Returning to our case study once more, perhaps there was an initial temptation for this newly appointed teacher to default to the way he himself was taught and, given the vocational area in which he was trained over many years, this may have been a 'safety-first' position.

Observation and experience would suggest that some teachers new to the LLS – and some who have not developed their style over time – tend to favour the direct style. One disadvantage of this approach is that it tends to encourage passivity in learners rather than motivating them to engage actively with their learning, and places most of the burden of responsibility for learning on the *teacher*. On the other hand, direct styles of teaching can work very well indeed when combined with other, more open and learner-centred approaches as part of a learning continuum.

Indirect teaching style

A gradual shifting of responsibility for learning to the learners themselves may require a more indirect teaching style. When in 'indirect mode', the teacher actively listens to learners through dialogue and other forms of interaction in order to create a transactional learning environment. Teaching methods should be aimed towards activity, both physical and experiential wherever possible, avoiding casting learners into a passive role or taking the form only of teacher 'input'.

There is of course a notion of *freedom* within the indirect style (Rogers and Freiberg, 1993), although this is not an approach that can be arrived at without careful planning and due consideration of learners and their own individual or preferred learning styles.

Differentiated techniques for teaching and learning are now often couched in terms of multiple intelligence theory (Gardener, 1993). However, it could be argued that, in practice, this treatment is often superficial with a danger that the mere notation of the various 'intelligences' on lesson plans are not attributed to individuals at all. A psychological approach such as this must be undertaken with caution and applied in an informed way if it is to be of any use in educational terms. The main consideration here is concerned with the accommodation of the diversity within the group. It should not, therefore, be simply a matter of covering all the bases, but rather of ensuring that individual needs are *understood and addressed.* The teacher's understanding of the theory that informs their teaching style must, therefore, be sound if it is to be applied effectively. This is a professional responsibility.

A more indirect teaching style is likely to raise issues of classroom management and the need to take into account the social dynamics within groups of learners. This is a vital element as it is important for LLS teachers to realise that, within the adult learning sector, their role is as much involved with the *facilitation and management of learning* as what could be recognised as 'teaching' – certainly in the didactic sense (Curzon, 2004, pp3–16).

Returning to our case study once more, let's imagine now that our teacher became aware, by looking at the advanced practices of his peers, that he was actually too formal and controlling in his approach and, as the levels of teaching varied, he saw the need to create more opportunities for learning and less *teaching*.

Key to this, and inextricably linked to choice of teaching method, is the classroom as environment and resource. What happens if the teacher's options are constrained by poorly laid-out or inappropriate learning environments? Tables set out in rows; seating which is arranged in such a way that some students are seated facing away from the teacher; rooms too small or irregularly shaped to allow for the rearrangement of classroom furniture: all of these can constrain, or even dictate, the teacher's choice of style and methods.

Are you teaching comfortably?

It is vital for developing professional educators to be able to discover in experiential terms the usefulness of varying teaching styles and the need to be able to vary their style according to the context and content of the curriculum, and the level of learner ability. Initial or default styles are often a result of the teacher's own experience of being a learner (Wallace, 2005, p82); and perhaps this tendency to default to the familiar has to be recognised by teachers themselves before development can be embraced fully.

Peer observation is an excellent method of identifying whether we are teaching in a way that is comfortable for ourselves rather than appropriate to the needs of our learners. It may tell us whether we are taking the risks necessary to develop our range of styles to meet the needs of our learners. Similarly, taking measures to elicit learner feedback is essential in order to provide us with indicators of our effectiveness as teachers. This aspect of personal development requires us to trust the judgements of others, and may involve us in taking a hard look at ourselves and the choices we are making in planning our approaches to teaching.

Sometimes a criticism of our teaching performance can be a difficult thing to accept. Reflecting on such feedback may initially make us feel very uncomfortable; but most teachers would agree that such feedback is necessary if we wish to learn how we might adapt and vary our styles of teaching.

On one occasion when I was working with a group of pre-service education students, a key issue around the notion of 'comfort' was raised by various learners within the group. Following an initial activity where the learners were required to conduct a 30-minute teaching exercise, a tutorial session revealed that these 'new' teachers had realised that, via peer assessment and general feedback, they had been operating within a very supportive and largely uncritical environment. The feedback had contained little in the way of constructive critique of the session and, therefore, had not necessarily been as useful to each learner as it might have been if detailed criticism around teaching style had been more forthcoming. Of course these were trainee teachers at the very beginning of their careers and very much within the formative stage, but it is interesting to note how frustrated they tended to be with platitude as opposed to indicators of specific routes to improvement.

'My feedback was very warm and kind – but not critical enough' said one.

The learners in this case found themselves safely in a zone of comfort, but realised that they needed exposure to more objective feedback on their performance – and were very open to the notion of receiving this.

Our own learners, by and large, will not be trained educators, but they are the most important people in the classroom, and their feedback is essential. Most FE institutions regularly survey learners in order to take into account the 'learner voice'. There are various ways of doing this. Some conduct learner satisfaction surveys to discover the level of satisfaction with the learning process in general, in order to gather quantitative data; while others gather qualitative data by way of focus groups or course committees.

Our case study of the engineering teacher moves forward now to a phase where he takes on a more varied range of teaching, moving beyond the topic-based to subjects and levels which require the teacher to become a facilitator of learning rather than a deliverer of knowledge. He learns to become a resource for supporting student learning, rather than the sole source of instruction. In other words he is becoming a professional educator.

Moving out of our comfort zones

As teachers we should be constantly engaged in a process of reflecting on our practice and, if necessary, making incremental changes to it. Making decisions on style is at the core of professional formation. But teachers are also individuals, and we must remember that learners, as well as benefiting from their teachers' ability to adjust and adapt their teaching approaches as necessary to the subject area and the learner needs, may very well value the differences in style between the different teachers who support their learning.

Conducting a self-audit of personal teaching style

In order to identify our own preferred or 'default' teaching style, it may be useful to undertake a self-audit, using the following approach.

Step 1

Conduct a comprehensive self-audit of all of the teaching that you are currently engaged in, including the levels, the context and the characteristics of your learners (for example, their ages, ability levels, prior experience and the intended outcomes of their study and any information you may have gathered about their preferred learning styles).

Step 2

Next you should reflect on the following questions.

- How am I going to motivate, or continue motivating, my students to learn?
- What would be a useful balance between requiring the learners to remember facts and encouraging them in the interpretation of knowledge?
- How can learning be expressed beyond competence?
- How much do I tell and how much should my learners find out for themselves?
- How much time should I allow my learners for active experimentation?
- How do I ensure that my learners can reflect on what they have achieved?
- What range of assessments can I use to measure what has been learned?
- How can I create an incentive for my learners to actively participate in learning?
- Do I encourage activities which allow me to use praise and applaud success?
- If I use learning styles surveys, do my learners understand what they mean?
- Do I understand what the results of learning styles surveys mean for teaching?
- Do I vary my style of teaching sufficiently to take the above into consideration?

Step 3

Is the feedback you receive on your teaching (for example, from your learners, your mentor, your tutor, your colleagues or peers) consistent with your own answers to these questions?

Conclusion

Our engineering teacher has moved on in his practice and now teaches across the curriculum in a teacher educator role. Although he did eventually become conscious of his own 'default' style and took steps to become more flexible and adaptable, this process would probably have taken far less time, and the outcome been more certain, if he had been required to engage in standards-based teacher education, as he would be, of course, if he were entering the profession today.

For anyone entering the teaching profession in the LLS it is essential that they should make a priority of developing professional self-awareness and due consideration of the needs – or learning styles – of learners. This may well involve them in moving out of their comfort zone; but it is the first essential step to developing a range or repertoire of teaching styles which will serve the learners' needs rather than their own.

References

Biggs, J (1999) *Teaching for quality learning at university*. Buckingham: Open University Press.

Coffield, F, Moseley, D, Hall, E and Ecclestone, K (2004) *Should we be using learning styles? What research has to say to practice.* Available: **www.lsnlearning.org.uk/search/Resource-32186.aspx**. (accessed November 2009).

Curzon, L (2004) Education teaching and learning, in Curzon, L *Teaching in further education: an outline of principles and practice*. London: Continuum.

DfES Standards Unit (2004) *Equipping our teachers for the future: reforming initial teacher training for the learning and skills sector*. London: HMSO.

Gardner, H (1993) *Frames of mind: the theory of multiple intelligences* (10th edn). New York: Basic Books.

Grasha, AF (1996) *Teaching with style: a practical guide to enhancing learning by understanding teaching and learning styles.* Pittsburgh, PA: Alliance Publishers.

Honey, P and Mumford, A (1992) *The manual of learning styles* (3rd edn). Maidenhead: Peter Honey.

Kolb, D (1984) *Experiential learning: experience as the source of learning and development*. Upper Saddle River, NJ: Prentice Hall.

Mosston, M and Ashworth, S (1990) *The spectrum of teaching styles from command to discover*. White Plains, NY: Longman.

Rogers, C and Freiberg, HJ (1993) *Freedom to learn* (3rd edition). New York: Merrill.

Wallace, S (2005) *Teaching and supporting learning in further education* (2nd edn) Exeter: Learning Matters.

Professional skills for reading and writing

This section aims to support and extend your understanding of the text, and to highlight some of the conventions of formal academic writing. It looks at style and tone; and the use of the first person, 'I'. It is designed to build your own confidence and skills as both a reader and writer of formal professional or academic texts.

1. Style and tone

You will have noticed that the style and tone of this paper is less formal than some of the others included in this book. For example, in places the author refers directly to his own professional experience. Some of the other features of this paper which create a less formal 'feel' are the use of the case study which encourages reader involvement by introducing an element of story-telling; the use of straightforward, everyday language; and the avoidance of very long paragraphs. In style as well as content the paper is clearly aimed more directly at practitioners than at a purely academic readership interested only in theory. Nevertheless, you will also have noticed that, like all good academic writing, it draws on relevant theory in order to support the points that are made; and it provides clear references to the literature cited.

2. Use of the first person 'I'

Many professionals new to academic writing in the field of education assume that it is bad practice to use the first person singular –'I' – in writing of this kind. This is not the case at all. Like other social sciences, education is a field in which much of the writing and research focuses on people. It is not an 'exact science'. The writer may well have a viewpoint, or be drawing on their own experience – as does the writer of the paper you have just read – and therefore cannot claim to be standing at an objective distance. Even when the writer is not telling their own story, it is still perfectly acceptable for them to write in the first person. Many people, and particularly those with a background in sciences or report writing, feel more comfortable using the third person passive (for example, not 'I decided . . .' but 'It was decided that . . .'). This, too, is perfectly acceptable. First person or third person: in writing about education this is usually a matter of your personal preference.

Discussion

DISCUSSION TASK

- If you used the suggested steps provided to help you to audit your own teaching style and preferences, what did you find? Did you identify any points for your own professional development?

- To what extent do the accommodation and the resources provided for your teaching facilitate or constrain the styles of teaching you adopt?

FURTHER READING FURTHER READING **FURTHER READING** FURTHER READING

You may find the following sources useful for following up the issues raised in this paper:

Collins, M (1991) *Adult education as vocation. A critical role for the adult educator*. London: Routledge.

Falchikov, N (2004) *Improving assessment through student involvement: practical solutions for higher and further education teaching and learning*. London: Routledge.

Maslow, A (1970) *Motivation and personality* (2nd edn). New York: Harper & Row.

Mason, J (2002) *Researching your own practice: the discipline of noticing*. London: Routledge/Falmer.

Race, P (2005) *Making learning happen. A Guide for Post Compulsory Education*. London: Sage.

Stenhouse, L (1975) *An introduction to curriculum research and development*. London: Heinemann.

Wallace, S (2007) *Teaching, tutoring and training in the Lifelong Learning sector*. Exeter: Learning Matters.

The following websites also provide material relevant to this chapter.

www.ifl.ac.uk/professional-standards
www.lsnlearning.org.uk/
www.geoffpetty.com/style.html
aeq.sagepub.com/cgi/content/abstract/35/4/220
www.lluk.org/documents/orientation-guidance-for-qualified-teachers-entering-further-education.pdf
tlp.excellencegateway.org.uk/teachingandlearning/
www.heacademy.ac.uk/assets/York/documents/resources/resourcedatabase/id477_aligning_teaching_for_constructing_learning.pdf

2

The origins and implications of the professional standards for teachers in the Lifelong Learning sector

The aims of this chapter are to provide:

- an example of academic writing style;
- a template for structuring a piece of academic writing;
- an overview of how policy has shaped the LLS and the role of the teacher;
- an explanation of the purpose of White Papers and Green Papers;
- an opportunity to distinguish between reasoned, balanced argument and writing which is designed to persuade (known as polemic or rhetoric).

What to look for

- As you read, make a note of any arguments which are presented and how these are distinguished from the factual information being offered.
- Notice how abbreviations and acronyms are presented.
- Look carefully at how references are made to other texts, and how these are set out.

Author details

Susan Wallace is Professor of Continuing Education at Nottingham Trent University. She is responsible for mentoring newly appointed staff in the School of Education, and has published extensively on the professional development of teachers and trainers.

The origins and implications of the professional standards for teachers in the Lifelong Learning sector

Susan Wallace

Abstract

This paper offers a critical analysis of the background to the introduction of the current professional standards for Qualified Teacher: Learning and Skills (QTLS). It provides an overview of the sector in terms of recent policies and the impact these have had on the professional development and practices of teachers within further education (FE) colleges and other Lifelong Learning sector (LLS) centres of provision. In doing so, it explores the question of how professional values can be assessed and discusses whether raising standards of teaching is alone sufficient to improve learner achievement.

Introduction

Since September 2001, it has been a requirement that all teachers in FE colleges and other centres of skills training within the LLS should have, or be working towards, a nationally recognised teaching qualification. The original professional standards upon which such a qualification was based were drawn up by the Further Education National Training Organisation (FENTO). In order to receive FENTO endorsement for their awards, universities and bodies such as the City and Guilds London Institute (CGLI) and the Royal Society of Arts (RSA), which at that time awarded a range of sector-specific teaching qualifications, were required to ensure that the content and outcomes of their teaching qualifications conformed to these professional standards. Only teachers with a FENTO-endorsed qualification were deemed to meet the national requirement for the profession.

As the result of a government policy change, the national training organisations, including FENTO, were replaced by sector skills councils, and responsibility for managing the professional standards and endorsing qualifications for teachers in LLS was taken over in January 2005 by Standards and Verification UK (SVUK), the standards and verification arm of Lifelong Learning UK (LLUK). This body, which is also responsible for the professional development of teachers in work-based learning and higher education (HE), brought out a revised set of professional standards in 2007, following a lengthy period of consultation. These are known as Qualified Teacher: Learning and Skills (QTLS) standards; and it is now a requirement that all teachers in the sector, whether full-time or part-time, must have, or be working towards, QTLS. This can be achieved by a number of routes, including SVUK-endorsed HE programmes such as the Certificate of Education (Cert Ed), the Postgraduate and Professional Graduate Certificates in Education (PGCE and ProfGCE), or a teacher training programme at National Qualification Framework (NQF) level 5 or 6 offered by one of the commercial unitary awarding bodies.

But what was the situation before 2001? What were the issues and policies which led to the development of the first set of national standards for teachers in FE? And what are the implications of the introduction of such standards? These are some of the questions which this paper now goes on to explore. In doing so, it aims to give a clear overview of the sector and clarify for teachers the contextual background of the sector in which they are working.

The rationale for the standards

It was in 1998 that the recommendation was made in the government Green Paper, *The Learning Age* (DfEE) that all teachers in the FE and skills training sector should be qualified to agreed national standards. A Green Paper is a consultative document, and therefore part of the purpose of *The Learning Age* was to invite responses to this recommendation from the sector itself and from relevant stakeholders. The argument used in the Green Paper to support the government recommendation was that in order to raise standards of achievement in the sector it was necessary to raise standards of teaching; and that to raise standards of teaching it was necessary to introduce professional standards by which teachers' performance could be measured. In other words, the introduction of the standards was presented as central to the success of a wider policy, which was to raise standards of teaching, learning and attainment in FE and skills training.

The argument was, on the surface, a strong one. Prior to the introduction of the initial standards in 2001, large numbers of teachers and trainers with no formal teaching qualifications were employed within the sector. There were historical reasons for this. Because of the sector's focus on specialised vocational and skills training, it tended to recruit as its teachers and trainers people who were subject specialists skilled in their own vocational area as expert hairdressers, plumbers, electrical engineers and so on. It was their expertise in their vocational skill which was sought, rather than professional teaching skills. This model, of the vocational expert transmitting skills and knowledge to trainees, was closely bound up with the traditional idea of apprenticeship and was therefore both familiar and accepted within the skills training sector. The teacher's acquisition of teaching skills, therefore, was often achieved 'on the job' simply through practice, or with the guidance of a line manager or mentor. Teacher training was usually voluntary and was undertaken on a part-time, in-service basis, leading to accreditation from an awarding body such as CGLI or from the Council for National Academic Awards (CNAA) through a polytechnic (the higher education institutions (HEIs)) which later (1992) were offered university status and became the 'new' universities. The introduction of the standards in 2001, therefore, not only imposed a requirement that all newly appointed teachers to the sector should have, or be training towards, an appropriate teaching qualification; but also that all existing teachers must now gain a qualification, regardless of how long or how successfully they had been teaching.

These were some of the reasons why the argument behind the 1998 Green Paper appeared compelling, suggesting that if all teachers in the sector were trained and qualified to an approved standard this would be sure to raise the overall standard of teaching within colleges and, as a result, improve 'output' in the form of learner achievement. Some academic commentators, however, have suggested that the logic of this argument is questionable, pointing out that even if it were possible to prove that training to standards will raise overall teacher performance, or that untrained teachers under-performed, it remains debatable whether low levels of learner achievement can be raised simply by improved standards of teaching. Let us look more closely at this last point by rephrasing the question about standards of teaching and learner achievement thus: If poor learner performance is the result of something other than inadequate teaching, what might that 'something other' be? Various answers have been offered to this question, including learners' lack of hope and motivation (Wallace, 2002); the lack of stimulation provided by the work-related curriculum (Reeves, 1995); the lack of importance attributed by some young people to occupational status and work (Ball et al, 2000); the belief of some learners that their education and training is designed simply to occupy their time while not in employment (Ainley and Bailey, 1997); and the widening of participation without a corresponding widening of opportunity (Ball, 2008). All of these argue that in order to effectively raise levels of learner motivation and attainment we must first address underlying social, political and economic patterns and practices. They do not, of course, argue that standards of teaching are unimportant, but rather that there are limits to what can be achieved by simply improving teaching performance without reference to the wider social context.

It could be argued that the introduction of standards has also contributed towards establishing the professional status of teachers in the sector. Indeed, there is great emphasis in the QTLS standards on the concept of 'professionalism', which is defined in two ways: the requirement to adhere to a professional code of good practice, and the need to comply with a set of professional values. This suggests that there is a moral or values-based element to being a professional, as well as a requirement to demonstrate skills to a national standard. However, it is clearly the case that the practical skills of the teacher, such as lesson planning, assessing student progress and recording student achievement, are much simpler to reliably assess than are the teacher's attitudes and values, which can only be inferred from the way they demonstrate these skills and from their interactions with students, colleagues and others. If we take as an example the requirement set out in the QTLS standards to provide for differentiation of outcome or activity when planning a lesson, we can see that this is an instance in which the teacher can demonstrate an observable skill (incorporating differentiation into their planning) which may be taken to imply their acceptance and approval of notions such as equality, inclusion and social justice; but could simply indicate their willingness to comply with requirements even though they do not espouse the values that underpin them. The notion of 'standards' which seek to measure values, therefore, is a problematic one.

How successive policies have continued to shape the teacher's role

Since 1998 and the publication of *The Learning Age*, successive government policies have continued to shape the role and working practices of teachers in the LLS. In 1999 the White Paper, *Learning to Succeed*, signalled the setting up of central and regional Learning and Skills Councils (LSCs), which would replace the Further Education Funding Council (FEFC) nationally as a source of funding for FE, and replace the Training and Enterprise Councils (TECs) as a local body for the strategic distribution of that funding to colleges and other providers in the sector. The funding policies of local LSCs (LLSCs), with their emphasis on outputs and performance indicators (PIs) in the form of recruitment, retention and achievement figures, often resulted in larger class sizes and in an increase in the teacher time spent on administrative tasks of recording, tracking and reporting (often referred to as 'paperwork', even when conducted online).

Like many policy implementations in the sector, the LSCs were relatively short-lived, and were replaced in 2008 by regional boards. During the lifetime of the LSCs, however, another influential White Paper set out policy which was to have a further impact on teachers in the sector. In 2002, *Success for All* set out a strategy of reform which emphasised the need for colleges to demonstrate greater levels of responsiveness, both to the needs of local employers and to the needs of individual learners, ensuring that the provision offered followed the recommendation of the Tomlinson Report (Tomlinson et al, 1996) in supporting and encouraging diversity and equality, and encouraging the development of e-learning in order to provide access to education and training for a wider range of potential learners. The impact of these policies of widening participation on teachers' professional practices was in some cases profound. This included an emphasis on lesson planning for differentiation and inclusion, and a drive to incorporate information communication technology (ICT) into teaching and learning over and above the minimum level demanded by key skills provision. Teachers were required to develop their ICT competence as an integral part of their professional practice and subject specialist skills.

Two subsequent policy initiatives were also to have a far-reaching influence on practices within the sector. The first were the outcomes of the 2003 Green Paper, *Every Child Matters*, which indeed had considerable impact on professional practice in every sector of education, focusing on the need for better communication and integrated action between all agencies, services and organisations involved in the support of young people, particularly those at risk. Similarly influential was the policy decision set out in the 2005 White Paper, *14–19 Education and Skills* (DfES), to improve the motivation of some 14–16-year-old learners by removing the requirement that they follow every part of the National Curriculum (NC) and allowing them instead to undertake part of their learning through vocationally related courses in colleges of FE. Additionally, this White Paper proposed the target that all young people should have a mastery of functional English and mathematics by the time they finished full-time education. It also made mention of 'vocational Diplomas' which were later to re-emerge as the Diplomas currently available for 14–19-year olds. As a result of the policies set out in this White Paper, many teachers in the LLS now found themselves required to teach learners in an age group (14–16) of which they had no previous professional experience, and which presented a new range of challenges. They also had to redesign their teaching in order to fully support the development of learners' functional skills.

A further refinement of the LLS teacher's role resulted from the recommendations of the Foster Report, *Realising the Potential: A review of the future role of further education colleges* (2005) which set out to define the key purpose of the FE sector as one of skills training. This definition was confirmed in the 2006 White Paper, *Further Education: Raising Skills, Improving Life Chances*, a government response to the Foster Report and one which approved the implementation of the Report's major recommendations. For some teachers in FE colleges, this marked an end to their interpretation of their role as that of liberal educators whose purpose was to support the development and encourage the potential of the whole learner rather than to help them hone only specific workforce related skills. Since then, the legislated changes heralded in the 2008 Education and Skills Act promise a further, radical impact on the role and practices of teachers in the LLS, signalling as they do the requirement for all young people to remain in education and training until the age of 18.

Conclusion

Thus it can be seen that the QTLS standards, as they currently exist, are built upon and reflect a series of policy initiatives over the past decade or so which have shaped the requirements of the teacher's role not only in terms of how they teach, but also what they teach, why they teach and who they teach. The standards themselves, with their emphasis on professionalism, communication, planning and assessing, and subject specialist expertise, are best understood in the context of these policies which continue to shape the sector and the working lives of the professionals within it.

References

Ainley, P and Bailey B (1997) *The business of learning: staff and student experiences of FE in the 1990s*. London: Cassell.

Ball, S (2008) *The education debate*. Bristol: The Policy Press.

Ball, S, Macrae, S and Maguire, M (2000) *Choice, pathways and transitions post-16: new youth, new economies in the global city*. London: RoutledgeFalmer.

DfEE (1998) *The learning age: a Renaissance for a new Britain*. London: HMSO. Available: **www.lifelonglearning.co.uk/greenpaper** (accessed November 2009).

DfES (2003) *Every child matters*. **www.dcsf.gov.uk/everychildmatters/publications/outcomescyp** (accessed January 2010).

DfES (2005) *14–19 Education and Skills*. London: HMSO. Available: **www.dfes.gov.uk/publications/ 14-19educationandskills** (accessed November 2009).

DIUS (2007a) *Further education: raising skills, improving life changes.* London: Department for Innovations, Universities and Skills.

Foster, A (2005) *Realising the potential. A review of the future role of further education colleges*. Annesley, UK: DFES Publications.

Reeves, F (1995) *The modernity of further eudcation*. Bilston: Bilston College Publications.

Wallace, S (2002) No good surprises: intending lecturers' preconceptions and initial experiences of further education. *British Education Research Journal*, 28(1): 79–93.

Professional skills for reading and writing

This section aims to support and extend your understanding of the text, and to highlight some of the conventions of formal academic writing. It looks at abbreviations and acronyms; summaries and abstracts; and the language of White and Green Papers. It is designed to build your own confidence and skills as both a reader and writer of formal professional or academic texts.

1 Abbreviations and acronyms

The Lifelong Learning sector (LLS) has its fair share (and some would say more than its fair share) of specialist terminology and abbreviations. Look again at the first paragraph of this paper. You will see that it introduces a number of names, abbreviations and acronyms which are then used several times subsequently throughout the paper. But notice in that first paragraph how these are presented when they occur for the first time. First the full name is given, and then this is followed by the abbreviation or acronym in brackets. For example:

- Qualified Teacher: Learning and Skills (QTLS)
  When the term is referred to again, only the abbreviated form is used. It is possible for the writer to do this because the abbreviation has already been clearly explained. This rule, therefore, is a useful one to remember.
- Give the full version at the first mention, immediately followed by the abbreviation in brackets. After that you can safely use the abbreviation whenever the term needs mentioning again.

2 Summaries and abstracts

Look again at the abstract with which this paper begins. The purpose of an abstract is to summarise the contents of the paper, usually by focusing only on key arguments or findings. This is useful for busy professionals or researchers, enabling them to see in just a few lines whether the paper will be relevant to their needs.

Think about the following questions.

- In your view, is this abstract an accurate summary of the paper?
- Are there any *key aspects* to the paper which it omits to mention?
- Have a go at summarising the first paragraph of the section of the paper headed 'How successive policies have continued to shape the teacher's role' on page 13 in not more than two sentences.
- Why do you think the ability to identify and summarise key points is an important professional skill for teachers?

3 White Papers and Green Papers

- Notice that upper case is used for both these types of government policy documents. It is important to remember this when you are writing about them yourself.
- White Papers set out the government's policy and their reasons for its introduction. When this policy is accepted by Parliament it becomes law; it is enacted: set out in an Act of Parliament.
- A Green Paper, on the other hand, is a consultative document in which the government sets out its proposed policy and requests a response from interested bodies and stakeholders. The policy may then be revised in the light of that response.
- The style of writing in these documents is specialised. Their 'arguments' are necessarily one-sided because they are designed to win our approval. They therefore do not provide, nor usually acknowledge the existence of, a counter-argument, and are not usually underpinned by any close reference to independent research. This sort of writing, which aims to persuade us to accept one particular point of view, is known as a *polemic*. The language it uses is called *rhetoric*. It is quite different from the style of writing we find in academic journals. When you yourself are writing about the policies set out in government documents such as these you should be careful not to simply imitate their style. As a professional, your reading and response should be analytical. You should always test their claims and ideas against your own professional experience.

Discussion

The discussion topics which follow will help you to explore the relevance of what you have read here to your own experiences and practice, and to support the development of reflection and critical analysis.

DISCUSSION TASK

The main purpose of this paper is to summarise information relating to the professional standards and suggest how policy has shaped the requirements made of teachers in the sector. It does, however, set out some arguments.

- Can you identify two of them?
- Choose one and draft a short paragraph arguing in support.
- Now draft another short paragraph in which you put up a counter-argument. You could begin it with the phrase, 'On the other hand, it could be argued that. . .'

This is one way to begin to build a critical analysis.

DISCUSSION TASK

- Consider how any *one* of the provisions contained within the 2006 White Paper, *Further Education: Raising Skills, Improving Life Chances,* has contributed to the shaping of your own institution's curriculum, structure and mission and how it has influenced your own professional practice.
- Using the website links, explore any *one* of the other White or Green Papers cited in this paper and discover what other policy changes it set out. Now consider the impact of these on your own practice and your working environment.

FURTHER READING FURTHER READING FURTHER READING FURTHER READING

You can follow up your reading of this paper by looking for papers specifically related to your specialist subject or to other issues of current relevance to your practice in one of the following journals, available in hard copy or online. For online access, contact your college librarian:

- *Research in Post-Compulsory Education*
- *The Journal of Vocational Education*

Discussions in papers published in journals are usually more current than those found in books. Keeping an eye on what the journals are publishing in relation to your subject is one of the best ways to keep updated.

You will also find it useful to read Chapter 10 in this book, which examines some of the same legislation mentioned in the chapter, but from the point of view of its impact on the college as an institution rather than on the teachers as individual practitioners.

Chapter 5 in this book also reviews some of the recent legislation, this time from the point of view of its impact on the teaching of literacy and numeracy.

Chapter 6 discusses the way that recent legislation and policy has shaped the qualification and assessment systems now in use in the LLS.

You should find that, taken together, these chapters provide a useful and detailed account of policy context and recent key developments in the sector.

In your further reading of journal papers, chapters and books, you may find it helpful to use what you have learned from this chapter to identify the key arguments being presented. It is also a good idea to pay particular attention to the language used. For example: Are the authors communicating their ideas clearly? Is the language they are using straightforward? This is just as important as ensuring the style is appropriate to an academic readership. If the language used cannot be understood, the writer has failed to communicate!

3
Are lesson plans important?

The aims of this chapter are to provide:

- an analysis of the lesson planning process;
- an analysis of the ways in which lesson planning is assessed within QTLS programmes;
- a worked example of how different theoretical frameworks can be drawn on to explore a research problem.

What to look for

- As you read, make a note of the ways in which the central argument, relating to the lesson planning process, is presented.
- Take note of the ways in which academic writing conventions are used in this chapter.

Author details

Jonathan Tummons is senior lecturer in education at Teesside University, where he is also course leader for the BA in Education Studies. He has written several books and articles on teaching, learning and assessment in FE and HE. He has worked with adult learners in HE for 15 years, and with trainee teachers for the learning and skills sector since 2003.

Are lesson plans important?

Jonathan Tummons

Abstract

This chapter offers a critical analysis of the assessment of lesson plans (a common feature of portfolio-based assessment on QTLS courses). Drawing on assessment theory, theories of literacy as social practice, and primary data gathered through interview-based research, the chapter argues that the writing of lesson plans does not always adequately capture the complex process of lesson planning. Consequently, the assessment of lesson plans in teacher education courses may not be valid or reliable.

Introduction

> I've...written lesson plans for times I've been observed. The rest of my lesson plans come in...the form of a notebook. I don't spend hours writing lesson plans, because I don't get paid to do that.
>
> (Kate, PGCE (QTLS) student, Nunthorpe College)

In just about every general teacher training textbook that might be found on the reading list for a QTLS-endorsed qualification, you will find a substantial section on lesson planning and writing lesson plans (Armitage et al, 2007; Gray et al, 2005; Hillier, 2005; Reece and Walker, 2007). This is hardly surprising: even the most world-weary FE college lecturer knows that it is important to spend time carefully thinking about the different components that make up a (hopefully) successful session. Moreover, QTLS textbooks are in broad agreement over what these components are. Typically, when planning a lesson, a tutor (or a trainee tutor) would need to think about:

- the specific aims of the session;
- how this session fits into the broader aims of the course or module as a whole;
- the subjects or topics to be covered during the session;
- the resources or equipment that will be available;
- the nature of the student group;
- the different activities that will be undertaken by the tutor and the students, which may include assessment activities;
- approximate timings for these activities.

While working through a checklist such as this (and several other textbooks have similar such lists, of varying degrees of detail), a number of issues occur. When thinking about resources and equipment, you will need to consider whether you have enough equipment, or whether you will have to structure the session in such a way that your students, while working in pairs, take turns with the equipment: in this case, you will need to ensure that other activities are prepared to keep everyone busy while they wait their turn. Very few FE colleges have enough milling machines in their engineering workshops to allow a group of 12 students to all be working on one at the same time. In a session where Information Communication Technology (ICT) is being used, it is sensible to make sure that all of the machines are switched on and (if possible) logged on before the session starts. Waiting for computers to warm up can be frustrating and if one machine crashes, the session might be disrupted. If you want your students to make some posters, perhaps as a formative assessment exercise, you need to make sure that you have enough pens, paper and adhesive. Dealing with issues such as these requires common sense, and a good level of awareness of the facilities that are available to you within the institution where you work.

Some planning issues require a different kind of professional knowledge. In order to plan appropriately for the session aims, the content and how it will fit into the course or module as a whole, you will need to be familiar with the curricular documents that have been supplied by the awarding body responsible for the course that you teach. Although a few tutors do get to design their own courses or otherwise exercise a degree of autonomy over course structure and content, most of us have to work within the confines of the paperwork supplied by City and Guilds, or Open College Network (OCN), or whichever awarding body we are working with. As such, our planning processes will require a good degree of familiarity with the requirements of the curriculum in terms of specified content, assessment criteria, key transferable skills and such like.

Other planning issues rest on more theoretical knowledge. A consideration of the nature of the student group, and how this will impact on the planning of the session, might lead to a discussion of preferred learning styles (although this is a controversial topic and needs to be reviewed critically), or of the ways in which the profile of the students, in terms of age, ethnicity, prior experience or ability, might impact on group dynamics. It might lead to a consideration of issues that affect student motivation, or behaviour (a particularly relevant issue for tutors who work with 14–16 students). The needs of students with seen or unseen disabilities will have to be accounted for. All of these issues might have an impact on the decisions that we make about which resources to use, how those resources might be designed, or which activities to try.

No matter how exhaustive the planning process, however, it is important to remember that the plan itself is not set in stone. By treating our plans as a series of cues or prompts, rather than a series of rigid instructions, as tutors we can be confident that we have spent time and effort thinking about what we are going to be doing with our students that day, while at the same time being aware of the need to be flexible during the session itself. We cannot always predict how our students will respond to an exercise or an activity, and we need to be prepared to change things if need be. A responsive, reflective practitioner will be aware of how successfully – or not – a session is proceeding, and will be able to adapt accordingly. This might involve changing the running order of a session, or allowing a discussion to continue beyond its planned time, or turning a tutor-led activity into one led by a student group. Even if the planning took a long time and a lot of effort, we need to be prepared to deviate from it should the behaviour and responses of the students so dictate.

From lesson planning to lesson plans

I've learned loads from my Cert Ed, about how to do lesson plans, how to do my schemes of work. So for your job it does actually benefit you.
(Rachel, Cert Ed (QTLS) student, Scarcroft College)

Planning a lesson is one thing; writing a lesson plan is another. It seems to me to be perfectly reasonable to plan a lesson by sitting down in front of a blank sheet of paper and (for example) using a mind-mapping technique to help think about all of the factors that we need to consider. Then, when actually teaching the session, I could have the mind map in front of me to help me make sure that I do not miss anything out. At one level, it appears almost instinctive to say that in an ideal world, I could write my lesson plan any way I like, so long as it worked for me. And so some tutors might put lots of detail in; others might only put a small amount. Some tutors might use a mind map; others might use a bullet point list.

Then again, why write out a lesson plan at all? If I am capable of keeping all of my ideas 'in my head', why spend time writing on paper what I have already decided to do with my students that day? If I am an experienced and knowledgeable tutor, I'm going to have a pretty good idea about what I will be doing with my students today, tomorrow and next week as well. I know which resources I will use, and which assignments they are working towards. Spending 15 minutes writing out two sides of notes before going to teach a session that will only last for 50 minutes anyway seems like a poor way of managing my time, especially when we consider how busy the life of a college tutor is. Both new and experienced tutors are only too aware of the amount of paperwork that is involved in the job. Why add to it?

In fact, there are two issues at work here. One is the need to actually write down a lesson plan. The other is the need to write it down in a format that is invariably determined by the college or adult education centre where we work. We shall consider each of these in turn.

Writing down lesson plans

There is a pretty straightforward justification for this: writing helps us to remember things. By this I mean that the process of writing is itself a meaning making process: as we write, we work things out and make sense of them. At the same time there is a practical benefit as well. Having a written plan helps us remember what we are going to do next. I, for one, invariably get caught up in interesting diversions based on student discussions and questions. Without a lesson plan (of some kind) I might forget to cover all of the issues that I need to cover that day. Written lesson plans also lend themselves to revisions and adjustments: it is a useful process to be able to mark up a lesson plan with notes as to what worked, and why, and what did not, or what might need to be changed if the session is to be delivered again but with a different student group (for example, when teaching the same module or unit to a 16–19 group during the day, and an adult group in the evening).

There is one rationale for producing written lesson plans which is arguably more controversial. Some authors (and, I am sure, many teacher trainers and college managers) have argued that session plans are very helpful if a substitute tutor has to cover a class for some reason. With a written plan, and perhaps a course file containing copies of handouts, worksheets, PowerPoint slides and such like, a substitute tutor can take over if the regular tutor suddenly becomes unavailable (Armitage et al, 2007; Hillier, 2005). At first glance, this seems to be a perfectly sensible procedure. But it is important to bear in mind that however extensive the planning documentation, there is no substitute for a tutor who is properly qualified in the subject that is being studied. One of the critiques of the FE workplace is that staff sometimes feel pressurised into covering, or even taking on for the longer term, courses in which they lack qualifications and expertise. As such, any workplace procedures that can be interpreted as encouraging or normalising such approaches need to be treated with caution (Avis et al, 2002; Shain and Gleeson, 1999; Tummons, 2009).

Finally, it is worth remembering that written lesson plans are important as sources of evidence for portfolio-based assessment on teacher-training courses. PGCE and Cert Ed courses, as well as Preparing to Teach in the Lifelong Learning Sector (PTLLS), Certificate in Teaching in the Lifelong Learning Sector (CTLLS) and Diploma in Teaching in the Lifelong Learning Sector (DTLLS) courses, invariably require the trainee to compile a portfolio of teaching resources. In among the handouts, worksheets and reflective diaries, lesson plans are an important form of evidence for such assessment (Brown, 1999; Klenowski et al, 2006).

Using official lesson plan templates

Several of the general QTLS teacher-training books have suggestions for how lesson plans should be arranged (Gray et al, 2005; Reece and Walker, 2007). Generally, they tend to suggest various kinds of tabular formats, with the written page divided into columns with headings such as: tutor activities, student activities, timings, resources, key skills coverage and the like. And in fact such templates are familiar to those of us who work or have worked in FE colleges and adult education centres. Many FE colleges have their own institutional lesson plan templates that are distributed to staff at training days or via a college intranet. Adult education providers such as local authorities (LAs) or the Workers' Educational Association also provide such templates.

At one level, such templates can be seen as useful. They tend to be divided into columns, and cover the kinds of topics and areas (activities, key skills, assessment, timings) that we have already discussed. They have another function as well: they serve as quality assurance (QA) documents. As such, keeping such documents up to date becomes part of a general

QA strategy. And, of course, they are required for scrutiny when a tutor is observed during teaching, perhaps by a curriculum manager or an OFSTED inspector.

Why lesson plans may not always be so useful after all, and why this has an impact on the assessment of trainee teachers

It's so difficult to plan a lesson because your numbers could be, you could have ten in a group and only two turn up. You know, you could be two minutes into the lesson and two kids start fighting...so your whole plan just goes out of the window.

(Tom, Cert Ed (QTLS) student, Scarcroft College)

As part of a larger body of research about the assessment of trainee teachers in further and adult education, I started to think about lesson plans more critically (although in themselves they had not initially been a central area of the inquiry). During interviews with QTLS students from four different FE colleges (from which the quotations that appear in this chapter are taken), I encountered different attitudes to writing lesson plans. For some students, it was a helpful process; for others, it was not. For some, writing lesson plans was useful to them both as tutors and as students (more than three-quarters of all QTLS students are studying part-time, and are already working as tutors). Writing lesson plans helped them to think about their teaching and they valued the feedback that the teacher trainers gave them. Other students understood why lesson plans were useful, but simply found them unhelpful, preferring to find their own way of doing things. Unfortunately, they still needed to write some 'proper' lesson plans for their portfolios and their observations. And other students found the entire process to be a distraction. For this group of students, writing lesson plans was simply an exercise in bureaucracy: more paperwork.

These findings then led me to consider the ways in which lesson plans are actually used, and by whom. We have already mentioned the use of lesson plans as quality assurance documents (when having an OFSTED inspection, for example), and as assessment documents (when compiling a teaching portfolio for a teacher-training course, for example). It was the role of the lesson plan in assessment that raised particular questions. Specifically, assessment *validity* was the issue for debate. For any assessment to be valid, it has to be (among other things), authentic. That is to say, when talking about portfolio-based assessment on a professional HE course (such as teacher training), the things that the student puts into the portfolio need to be authentic documents and papers drawn from their workplace that represent accurately and sufficiently the workplace practices of the student (Cotton, 1995; Smith and Tillema, 2003; Tummons, 2007).

Therefore, if we are to assume that the assessment of a trainee teacher's portfolio is valid, it follows that (among other things) all of the documents that the trainee puts into the file are genuinely representative of the work that they have been doing as a tutor. A straightforward example would be a hard copy of a set of PowerPoint slides. If a student included a set of slides as a piece of evidence from an observed teaching session but had not actually used those slides, then the assessment of those slides *would not be valid*. For a student to say that they *might* have used the slides is insufficient. The slides may be able to be used in a different part of the portfolio, but not as evidence from the observed session, because those slides were not used during the session.

When thinking about lesson plans, this same principle applies, although the argument is a little more complex. For those students who find writing lesson plans and receiving feedback about them helpful, the assessment of those plans is a straightforward process. But for those students who do not write lesson plans as part of their normal working practice, the assessment of the plans becomes more problematic. If the lesson plan has only been put together because the portfolio requires it, rather than because the student actually finds it useful or helpful, is the assessment still valid? If the student normally does not write them, do they count as part of that student's normal, authentic working practice? Are we assessing the student's ability to plan a session, or a student's ability to write a lesson plan using an appropriate format?

Understanding what we're seeing

This was an agriculture module about livestock, and no offence to either of my teachers, but they know nothing about livestock...

(Louanna, PGCE (QTLS) student, Nunthorpe College)

If assessment validity is called into question by the nature of the lesson plans that are being assessed, then assessment *reliability* is called into question once we start to consider who actually reads and assesses them. For any assessment to be reliable, it needs to be consistent and repeatable. That is to say, if the same student did the same assessment but with two different assessors, the same result would be given every time. The outcome of an assessment decision (that is, whether the assessment is a pass or a fail) must not depend on the marker, but must rest on an objective decision. Reliable assessment also makes certain assumptions about the person doing the marking: most importantly, that they are qualified (in terms of knowledge, experience, expertise as well as certificates) to be making an assessment decision.

Much teacher training for the post-16 sector is generic. Apart from specialist qualifications for teachers of adult literacy and numeracy, Preparing to Teach in the Lifelong Learning sector (TLLS)/Certificate in Teaching in the Lifelong Learning sector (CTLLS)/Diploma in Teaching in the Lifelong Learning sector (DTLLS) awards are not subject specific. Teacher training groups have a mix of students who work in quite diverse teaching contexts, across many subject areas and institutional sectors. Teacher trainers are themselves a diverse group. As such, it is not uncommon for a trainee teacher to be observed by someone who is in no way an expert – or perhaps even vaguely knowledgeable – in the subject being taught. Now, some aspects of lesson planning are universal: the pacing and sequencing of activities; the appropriate and effective use of resources; the use of appropriate question-and-answer techniques, for example. An observer who is not necessarily an expert in the subject being taught can still make a legitimate assessment decision about factors such as these.

Lesson plans are not exhaustive documents: they rest, in part, on a great deal of implicit knowledge (Hillier, 2005). That is to say, they work as planning documents because of what the person who wrote the plan actually knows. If the tutor who is assessing the lesson plan knows the same kinds of things as the student who wrote it, if they share the same or a similar level of subject expertise, then this helps the reliability of the assessment process: the tutor has the expertise needed to make a reliable assessment decision. (This shared expertise is referred to as *assessor–assessee intersubjectivity* (Baume and Yorke, 2002)). But if the tutor shares little or no subject expertise or experience with the student being observed, are they still able to make a reliable assessment decision? Does a teacher trainer with a background in the humanities know enough to make a reliable assessment decision about the lesson plan drawn up by a tutor of electrical installation?

Summing up the issues and forming the argument

From the starting point of evaluating a series of responses made by students during interviews, therefore, a number of themes emerge.

- There is a consensus in the teacher training literature about those issues that need to be considered when drawing up a lesson plan.
- There is also consensus regarding the benefits of the planning process.
- There is a difference between lesson planning, and writing a lesson plan.
- Tutors do not all approach writing a lesson plan in the same way. Some prefer a more personalised approach, rather than using an institutional lesson plan template.
- The assessment of lesson plans, if it is to be valid, makes certain assumptions about those lesson plans: that they are an authentic representation of a tutor's work.
- The assessment of lesson plans, if it is to be reliable, makes certain assumptions about the expertise of the assessor as well as of the student.

In order to begin the process of turning these issues into a coherent academic argument, in the form of a paper for a conference or a journal, however, a few more theoretical strands need to be explored, drawing on appropriate academic literature. So far, a number of relevant theoretical approaches to the assessment process have been used and referred to. What is also needed is an appropriate theoretical framework that allows us to investigate the lesson plan as a written artefact, as a piece of paper. By this I mean that the issues of authorship and readership that we have hinted at above, need more systematic analysis. Questions such as why some people prefer to use their own notes whereas others prefer to use an institutional template, or why some people only do a plan if they are being observed and resist doing them the rest of the time, or why it is that different people will read the lesson plans in different ways and interpret them differently, also need to be theorised. An appropriate theoretical framework for doing this is the *New Literacy Studies* (NLS) (Barton 1994; Barton and Hamilton 1998).

Theorising the interview data

The New Literacy Studies (NLS) is a term used to describe a particular approach to thinking about literacy. Writers and researchers who draw on the NLS approach focus on the ways in which different people use literacies in different places. For example, the kind of literacies used by a trainee teacher (writing essays, writing reflections, having to use Harvard referencing) are quite different to the kinds of literacies used by an apprentice engineer (reading installation instructions, technical drawing) or by a catering and hospitality apprentice (reading recipes, writing menus, dealing with invoices and order forms in a busy kitchen) (Ivanic et al, 2009). According to the NLS approach, there are many kinds of literacy that are found in different walks of life: at work, at college and at home. Two relevant examples are *academic literacies* (Lillis, 2001, Tummons, 2008) and *workplace literacies* (Belfiore et al, 2004). Finally, it is important to note that some 'official' literacies are given more importance than other 'unofficial' literacies. For example, when writing essays, trainee teachers have to use a certain 'style' of writing: writing an essay in 'text message' English would not be approved of. These kinds of literacies are referred to as *dominant* and *vernacular* literacies (Barton and Hamilton, 1998, p10).

So how can these concepts help us to make sense of the interview data? Throughout this chapter I have used short, representative quotes from some of the interviewees, all of whom were trainee teachers working towards QTLS, to illustrate the different ways in which students approach writing their lesson plans. *Kate* (quoted at the beginning of the chapter) only did lesson plans when she had an observation. Her 'real' lesson plans were done in an A4 notebook that she carried with her all the time. Here, the official lesson plan is an example of a *dominant literacy practice*. Her use of a notebook is an example of a *vernacular literacy practice*. In contrast to this, *Rachel* was quite happy to use formal, official lesson plans, and found it beneficial to both her work and her studies. *Tom* meanwhile spent very little time writing plans of any kind because the nature of the student group with whom he works made planning so difficult. He simply did not know from one session to the next how they would behave, or even how many would be there. This is not to say that he did no planning at all: quite the opposite. But what he did do was plan a range of activities, and decide on the day, once the session was underway, what he would do. *Louanna* raised a different issue. She was concerned that the feedback that she had been given on one of her lesson plans, by a tutor who did not observe the lesson in question and had no background in Louanna's teaching area, simply did not understand the particular issues and pressures that she was planning for and effectively failed to understand what the lesson plan was all about.

Conclusion

To conclude, therefore, it can be argued that the writing of a lesson plan is in fact a complicated process, carried out for different reasons by different people. Moreover, the lesson plan does not reflect the process of lesson planning in a straightforward manner. Consequently, the assessment of lesson plans is problematic. If a lesson plan does not reflect the working practices of a trainee teacher, can the same lesson plan be seen as an authentic, and therefore valid component of a portfolio? And if the assessor who reads it does not understand fully what the lesson was actually about, can they make a reliable assessment decision about that lesson plan?

References

Armitage, A, Bryant, R, Dunnill, R, Flanagan, K, Hayes, D, Hudson, A, Kent, J, Lawes, S and Renwick, M (2007) *Teaching and training in post-compulsory education* (3rd edn). Maidenhead: McGraw Hill/Open University Press.

Avis, J, Bathmaker, A-M and Parsons, J (2002) Communities of practice and the construction of learners in post-compulsory education and training. *Journal of Vocational Education and Training*, 54(1): 27–50.

Barton, D (1994) *Literacy: An introduction to the ecology of written language.* Oxford: Blackwell.

Barton, D and Hamilton, M (1998) *Local literacies: reading and writing in one community.* London: Routledge.

Baume, D and Yorke, M (2002) The reliability of assessment by portfolio on a course to develop and accredit teachers in higher education. *Studies In Higher Education*, 27(1): 7–25.

Belfiore, M, Defoe, T, Folinsbee, S, Hunter, J and Jackson, N (2004) *Reading work: literacies in the new workplace.* New Jersey: Lawrence Erlbaum Associates.

Brown, S (1999) Assessing practice, in Brown, S and Glasner, A (eds.) *Assessment matters in higher education: choosing and using diverse approaches.* Buckingham: Open University Press/Society for Research into Higher Education.

Cotton, J (1995) *The theory of assessment: an introduction*. London: Kogan Page.

Gray, D, Griffin, C and Nasta, T (2005) *Training to teach in further and adult education* (2nd edn). Cheltenham: Nelson Thornes.

Hillier, Y (2005) *Reflective teaching in further and adult education* (2nd edn). London: Continuum.

Ivanic, R, Edwards, R, Barton, D, Martin-Jones, M, Fowler, Z, Hughes, B, Mannion, G, Miller, K, Satchwell, C and Smith, J (2009) *Improving learning in colleges: rethinking literacies across the curriculum*. London: Routledge.

Klenowski, V, Askew, S and Carnell, E (2006) Porfolios for learning, assessment and professional education in higher education. *Assessment and Evaluation in Higher Education*, 31(3): 267–86.

Lillis, T (2001) *Student writing: access, regulation, desire*. London: Routledge.

Reece, I and Walker, S (2007) *Teaching, training and learning: a practical guide* (6th edn revised). Sunderland: Business Education Publishers.

Shain, F and Gleeson, D (1999) Under new management: changing conceptions of teacher professionalism and policy in the further education sector. *Journal of Education Policy,* 14(4): 445–62.

Smith, K and Tillema, H (2003) Clarifying different types of portfolio use. *Assessment and Evaluation in Higher Education*, 28(6) 625–48.

Tummons, J (2007) *Assessing learning in the Lifelong Learning sector* (2nd edn). Exeter: Learning Matters.

Tummons, J (2008) Assessment, and the literacy practices of trainee PCET teachers. *International Journal of Educational Research*, 47(3): 184–91.

Tummons, J (2009) *Curriculum studies in the Lifelong Learning sector*. Exeter: Learning Matters.

Professional skills for reading and writing

This section is designed to provide you with guidance on writing up research. Having analysed the data, synthesised an appropriate theoretical framework and referred these discussions to other previously published research (which helps to provide a context for this analysis), the arguments presented in this chapter are now ready for writing up as a formal research paper for a conference or an academic journal. It is perhaps appropriate to note briefly that the way in which a research paper is written is quite different from the way in which a chapter in a QTLS textbook is written. They involve different *genres* or types of writing. In comparing an article from an academic journal (such as *The Journal of Vocational Education and Training* or *Research in Post-Compulsory Education*) to a textbook (such as this one), both the writing style and use of language (particularly specialist language, or jargon) will be different. Moreover, some of the issues discussed in this chapter will only be touched on briefly in the paper (for example, the actual process of lesson planning), while other issues (for example, the theoretical frameworks used to form the argument) will receive more detailed consideration. And some issues (such as research methods) will not appear in a chapter such as this at all, but will be important features of the research paper. We shall briefly discuss these points in order to illustrate how the content and writing of the paper will differ from this chapter.

The process of and assessment of lesson planning

As this chapter is to be read (primarily) by QTLS students, a discussion of the actual process of lesson planning, together with examples drawn from real-life case studies, is entirely appropriate. In the research paper, intended primarily for a scholarly audience, the process of lesson planning is not important: it is the assessment of lesson planning that is central. As such, the process of assessment will receive more detailed analysis in the research paper than in this chapter.

Theoretical frameworks

In a research paper, it is important for the author to demonstrate sufficiently that they have drawn on appropriate theoretical frameworks to ensure that the data and analysis that are being presented carry conviction. Therefore, issues surrounding assessment validity and reliability, and issues relating to the NLS perspective, will have to be presented comprehensively, although still briefly (the paper will not be much longer than this chapter). In order to keep this section of the research paper brief, an economical writing style, together with extensive referencing, will need to be used. In this chapter, the same theories have been drawn on, but with considerably fewer references. At the same time, theories are discussed in this chapter using less specialist language, which takes longer, but renders the discussion more accessible to a non-specialist readership.

Research methods

At several points in this chapter, quotations from interviews with QTLS students have been used to illustrate the points being made. When carrying out educational research, the ways in which interviews are conducted and then analysed are extremely important to the effectiveness and trustworthiness of the research as a whole. Therefore, in the research paper, some time must be spent explaining how the research was carried out, and how the findings of the research have been analysed.

Discussion

These discussion topics will help you to explore the relevance of what you have read here to your own experiences and practice, and to support the development of critical analysis.

DISCUSSION TASK

The main purpose of this paper is to explore the validity and reliability of the assessment of lesson plans. In order to do this, a broader discussion about assessment validity and reliability is also necessary. To what extent might these questions about assessment validity and reliability be extended to include other aspects of portfolio-based assessment? If you work with students who also have to compile portfolios as part of their studies, might the issues raised in this chapter apply to your own assessment decisions?

DISCUSSION TASK

The New Literacy Studies (NLS) framework is used here in quite a specific manner, as a theoretical tool for exploring how lesson plans are written, read and understood. This approach can also be applied to a much wider range of issues relating to literacy. (The book by Ivanic et al (2009), referenced above, is the first book-length exploration of this approach that directly relates to FE colleges and as such is highly recommended.) How might this approach be used to explore the literacy practices of not just QTLS students, but college life at large? The paperwork involved in the FE workplace can be bewildering. But what does it actually do? Who reads which kinds of form or report, and who has to write them? How does such paperwork shape or constrain the working lives of FE tutors?

FURTHER READING FURTHER READING **FURTHER READING** FURTHER READING

The references list that appears above will provide plenty of scope for follow-up reading. A range of sources is included: textbooks, scholarly monographs and academic journals. The research that is discussed here has indeed been written up as a research paper, which was presented by the author at the *British Educational Research Association (BERA)* conference in September 2008. The paper was subsequently accepted for publication in *Assessment and Evaluation in Higher Education* as:

Tummons, J (2009) The assessment of lesson plans in teacher education: a case study in assessment validity. *Assessment and Evaluation in Higher Education*.

4

Teaching for inclusion: pedagogies for the 'sector of the second chance'

The aims of this chapter are to provide:

- an example of academic writing style;
- an outline of the context in which FE has developed, and how it came to be regarded as the second chance sector;
- an overview of contemporary critiques of the second chance sector;
- a brief outline of the current policy context and an outline of how this has impacted on notions of the second chance sector;
- a consideration of some different pedagogical models and approaches associated with the sector.

What to look for

- Look carefully at the references to other texts and see how different types of citation are set out.
- When you have finished this chapter, revisit the original aims. Did it meet those aims?
- Look at how the chapter is divided into sections using subheadings and how each section relates to the previous one.

Author details

Liz Atkins spent 13 years managing and teaching on vocational education programmes in FE colleges and also has extensive experience as an educator of teachers in the LLS. Her published work focuses on in/equalities in education and the experience of students under-taking vocational programmes. She is currently Principal Lecturer in Learning and Skills at Nottingham Trent University.

Teaching for inclusion: pedagogies for the 'sector of the second chance'

Liz Atkins

Abstract

This chapter considers the notion of inclusion, and of a 'second chance' education and its associated pedagogies. Presented in four key sections, it begins with an overview of the sector, going on to discuss the concept of second chance in the context of contemporary literature and theories of second chance. It finds a strong association between social class and second chance education. The chapter then moves on to a discussion of different pedagogical theories and approaches currently associated with the sector, again considering them in the context of contemporary literature. It concludes that, in the current climate, second chance all too often means second best.

Introduction

The notion of a second chance education and theories around pedagogy are inherently political. They raise important questions such as what led a person to need a second chance? What should a good second chance education look like? Often the answers to such questions are inextricably linked to issues of social justice. For example, those who come to the sector for a second chance are often the socially excluded: students who may be regarded as less equal or marginalised in some way. By this, I mean those who have not achieved at school, or who experience particular characteristics associated with social and educational exclusion such as social class, race, gender or disability.

The purpose of 'inclusion' is to try to provide a 'level playing field' for those people who have been – for whatever reason – excluded from education. However, there are disagreements about the best way to achieve this, and whether some initiatives, pedagogies or curricula are empowering or disempowering.

Inclusion and social justice

Much of the writing about the FE and Lifelong Learning sector, including both academic work and government reports, refers to theories of social justice. This is a contested concept which has changed over time and has many different meanings, often according to individual values and perspectives. Morwenna Griffiths, a contemporary expert on social justice, paraphrases Ghandi in her argument that *social justice is not the end, it is the way* (Griffiths, 1998, p12). In a later book (2003, p55) she emphasises this idea of social justice being active in her argument that *social justice is a* **verb** (original emphasis). Similarly, Walker has argued that *only through doing justice can we make justice* (quoted in Griffiths, 2003, p125). These, and similar arguments, emphasise both the potentially transforming nature of education on people's lives and the need for all educators to engage in a fight for social justice and ensure that all their students are offered equitable opportunities in life and education.

These ideas of equity and transformation are important in the context of inclusion. Inclusion is often interpreted by teachers in purely instrumental terms such as giving a dyslexic student coloured handouts. This is not inclusion. Inclusion is about providing an *equitable* learning experience for students and about acknowledging and valuing all the differences that make us unique, as well as being related to broader aspects of social exclusion. However, in considering theories and notions of inclusion we must not forget that most students in the LLS fall at the bottom of a societal stratification which constitutes *layers* of inclusion and not just a distinction between inclusion and exclusion (Bathmaker, 2005). The theories and concepts around both inclusion and social justice are complex, but are particularly relevant in the LLS with its historical association with second chance education.

The Lifelong Learning sector

The Lifelong Learning sector, and more particularly FE colleges, have their roots in the evening classes which evolved for workers in the late nineteenth century. These were followed by the development of technical colleges serving local industrial needs in the early twentieth century, and eventually the provision of FE was made a statutory require-ment in the 1944 Education Act.

The sector continued to develop and diversify, and during the 1970s and 1980s was regarded very much as a second chance for those who had not achieved at school or who wished to return to education as adults. Provision for students with special needs began to be established around this time, and Access courses for adults who had not achieved at school were also established, with the aim of offering them a 'second chance' to gain entry to HE (Bailey, 2002, p67). At this time the FE sector was confined to FE, then under LEA control, which offered a broad range of technical and work related courses as well as subjects which fell under the heading of 'liberal studies' or 'general education'.

During the 1980s mass youth unemployment led the government to establish training schemes for young unemployed people which were managed by the now defunct Manpower Services Commission (MSC) and which offered four days a week in work and one day a week of 'off the job' training. Most of this training was provided by the colleges, and introduced to them a new cohort of young people, who in earlier times would have made a transition from school to (largely unskilled) employment. Other initiatives such as the Certificate in Pre-vocational Education (CPVE), which was also offered in schools, were established at this time and this approach to education became known as the 'new voca-tionalism'. Subsequent developments included the work related National Vocational Qualifications (NVQs), and subsequently the General National Vocational Qualification (GNVQ), a broad vocational qualification introduced in 1992. At around the same time, as a result of changes announced in the 1991 White Paper, colleges were released from LEA control and became semi-autonomous, receiving funding from the Further Education Funding Council (FEFC), and later the Learning and Skills Council (LSC). This led to a more managerialist and finance driven sector.

More recently, what has now become a highly diversified sector operating not only in colleges, but also across a whole range of other providers, has been the subject of a whole raft of government policies and initiatives which have focused funding on 14–19 vocational education with the implementation of initiatives such as the specialised Diploma. As a consequence, funding priorities now mean that skills-based courses such as NVQs may be readily accessed, but that other programmes, such as language conversa-tion courses which people might have taken for interest, or, more importantly, programmes such as the community-based courses which once formed a key access route back into education for those seeking a second chance, are often now available only at a cost to the student. This has had a significant impact on adult learning in particular and means that many of those most in need of a second chance, who lack the confidence or pre-requisite credentials necessary for skills-based programmes, may be unable to access education as the financial cost of courses may well be beyond their means.

Second chance

As noted above, the notion of FE as offering a second chance has been prevalent since the 1970s, is regarded as such by many teachers in the sector (Bathmaker and Avis, 2005) and is written into the Professional Standards in the context of *encouraging learners to seek initial and further learning opportunities* (LLUK, 2006, p14). The sector is also seen as a second chance by many of the students accessing it (for example, see work by Bathmaker, 2001, p94 and by Ross and Gray 2005, p103). However, changes in policy and funding priorities have led to a reduction in the availability of many adult education courses and to an emphasis on skills-based programmes which may not be appropriate for all, and more importantly may not lead to the outcomes individuals aspire to. It can be argued that this leads to a denial of opportunity. Furthermore, the perceived quality and value of much of the broad vocational training available in the sector has led to academic criticisms of the contemporary vocational curriculum as being not *second chance, but second best* (Bathmaker, 2001, p94). Bathmaker supports her argument with interview data from students which *suggest[s] that they perceive GNVQ as a second chance qualification, but not of equal status to academic qualifications* (ibid, p94).

Similarly, criticisms of HE provision offered by FE colleges as part of the widening participation agenda have suggested that this, too, may be a second best option. For example, Hayward et al's ongoing study has shown that students with combinations of vocational and academic qualifications are more likely to access HE successfully than those holding only vocational qualifications (Hoelscher and Hayward, 2008, p20). In addition, Vocational Education and Training (VET) students are more likely to attend less selective HE institutions. Hoelscher and Hayward go on to argue that this has significant implications for the introduction of the specialised Diploma, particularly in terms of accurate advice and guidance, an issue also raised by Colley et al (2008).

Other literature, which explores the notions of *learning careers* and *learning identities* helps to explain the importance of a second chance education. Government papers use rhetoric emphasising *choice* and *opportunity* but this tends to treat progression and straightforward transition as the same thing. However, research suggests that, rather than being straightforward, individual choices and trajectories are highly complex, and subject to significant influence by and interaction with local job market opportunities (Hodkinson et al, 1996; Ball, et al 2000; Bloomer and Hodkinson, 2000; Hodkinson and Bloomer, 2001). Hodkinson, et al (1996) developed the theory of *horizons for action* to explain how, for young people, their career choices are constrained by what is available (in the jobs or education market) and by their subjective perceptions of what is, or is not, suitable for them. Also writing in 1996, Hodkinson explored transformations of identity, and proposed the notion of *careership*, rejecting the concept of rational *ladder-like* trajectories. The concept of careership proposes the notion of development as transformation, based on turning points (Hodkinson, 1996, pp132–133).

Hodkinson's work relates mainly to youth transitions, and this and other work shows that for many young people, a decision to leave education at 16 or 18 may be followed by a 'turning point' which leads them back into education. Similar research among adults returning to education has had similar findings. Crossan et al drew on Hodkinson's ideas in their study of adults and concluded that:

> *Our model of learning careers involves recognition that learning careers are contradictory and volatile. They do not travel in one direction alone, but can go into reverse, not once but many times.*
>
> *An explicit rejection of education may form a deeply rooted and recurring component of some individuals' sense of themselves and their place in the world. Yet these non-participant identities may coexist with episodic participation and with values which favour educational achievement in children. Learning careers are, then, frequently complex and multi-directional, just as learning identities may*

be extremely fragile and vulnerable to sudden changes in the learner's immediate social milieu.

(2003, p65)

Other authors have considered the wider benefits of participation in second chance education. Reporting on an Australian study, Ross and Gray (2005, p103) argue that *re-entry into second chance education is a personal act of agency through which young people struggle to reclaim successful personal and educational identities amidst the constraints and hazards in their daily lives*.

Ross and Gray's study also illustrates the fact that the second chance sector is also *class specific* (Colley et al, 2003, p479; Macrae et al, 1997, p92). This means that those people who access vocational programmes are mainly from lower socio-economic or 'working-class' groups and as such, are disproportionately affected by other exclusionary characteristics such as disability, race and gender. Social class is a powerful determinant of life chances from the time a person is born, and mediates (or influences) all other exclusionary characteristics. In view of these constraints, these are the groups who are most likely to 'fail' during secondary education and later, to seek a second chance in the FE sector.

Other influences on the value of a second chance education include the policy and managerialist constraints under which both staff and students work. These were eloquently described by Hodkinson et al, who stated that:

When we look at all 17 sites over the 3 years of the fieldwork, it is hard to identify major policy or managerial initiatives which contributed to the improvement of learning in any site.

(2007, p403)

This point emerges, too, in earlier work such as that by Avis (2007); Bathmaker (2006) and Randle and Brady (1997a and 1997b) which associates these constraints with the deprofessionalisation of teachers in the sector. This has also been associated with increasing intensification of their workload (usually in terms of administration) together with diminished control over their work (Esland, 1996, p33; Ainley and Bailey, 1997, p62). This diminished control also extends to the curriculum offered within the sector.

Centralised control of the curriculum can be dated back to the establishment of the MSC, the Youth Training Scheme (YTS) and Youth Opportunities Programme (YOP) of the 1980s. Today, not only is the curriculum centrally prescribed, whereby NVQs, Business and Technology Education Council (BTEC) awards, Basic Skills programmes and the specialised Diploma are taught and assessed to centrally determined, fixed criteria, but the way in which the curriculum is delivered is also increasingly controlled. Until recently, although teachers were constrained by a central curriculum, it could be argued that *In practice, courses are greatly affected by what tutors and students bring to the situation and by the negotiations which ensue between them, and are not simply a result of some central prescription of the learning experience* (Bloomer, 1998, p177). More recently, however, specific pedagogical approaches have been determined, either centrally, as in the policy recommendation that 'personalisation' of learning should be implemented, or through the expectations of OFSTED that particular approaches such as the assessment of learning styles should be used, effectively making this common practice across most of the sector. These different pedagogical models and approaches are critiqued below.

Pedagogic theories

The term pedagogy has its roots in the Greek word *paidagogos* which referred to a slave who took a child to school. It is now taken to mean *the profession, science, or theory of teaching* (*Oxford English Dictionary*, 2003, p832). The word pedagogue has come to have a pejorative meaning, and refers to a *strict or pedantic* teacher (ibid). During the twentieth century, the word pedagogy was particularly associated with the education of children, although it is now used in a wider sense. Partly as a response to this, some work on the education of adults used a different term – andragogy. Much of this work was carried out by Malcolm Knowles, whose work in the mid-twentieth century was heavily influenced by that of Carl Rogers, the psychologist who developed the concepts of client-centred therapy and student-centred learning. The term andragogy may be traced back to as long ago as the early 1800s, but was brought into common usage by Knowles. Knowles believed that the teaching of adults should be predicated on four, later five assumptions about adults (which are different to the assumptions on which the practice of teaching children is based). His five assumptions (six, if you count his assumption that all persons are male!) are as follows.

- Self-concept: *as a person matures his self concept moves from one of being a dependent personality toward one of being a self-directed human being.*
- Experience: *as a person matures he accumulates a growing reservoir of experience that becomes an increasing resource for learning.*
- Readiness to learn: *as a person matures his readiness to learn becomes oriented increasingly to the developmental tasks of his social roles.*
- Orientation to learning: *as a person matures his time perspective changes from one of postponed application of knowledge to immediacy of application, and accordingly his orientation toward learning shifts from one of subject-centredness to one of problem centredness.*
- Motivation to learn: *as a person matures the motivation to learn is internal.*

(Knowles, 1984, p12)

The work of Knowles has been subject to criticism. For example, his theory assumes that all adults will display the characteristics listed above, and while recognising that different approaches might be needed in the teaching of adults, it draws heavily on opposing psychological models and lacks clarity in terms of a conceptual framework. Smith (1999) has reviewed these criticisms. His discussion, together with further reading may be found at: **www.infed.org/lifelonglearning/b-andra.htm**.

Knowles's theory is concerned with the characteristics of learners. A very different pedagogical model, critical pedagogy, is more concerned with changes in consciousness. Notions of critical pedagogy, which refer to approaches concerned with working with students to enable them to understand and question oppressive and dominating structures in society and education (such as race, gender and class, for example), are drawn from the work of Paolo Freire. Freire was a Brazilian academic and teacher who experienced poverty and recognised the transformational nature of education. In 1968 his work *Pedagogy of the Oppressed* was published. He has since been associated with teaching for social justice, something which is of great importance in a sector which is associated in many minds with a second-class education (Bathmaker, 2001, p94) for students drawn predominantly from lower socio-economic groups (Colley et al, 2003, p 479), many of whom experience *multiple oppressions* (Atkins, 2009, p47) in their daily lives. It is difficult to summarise Freire's theories into techniques which might be used in the classroom, since he advocated critical thought and was very concerned that his ideas might become a method which was followed uncritically. He was opposed to transmission theories and practices of education and considered that an emancipatory curriculum must grow out of lived experience and social circumstances (Flinders and Thornton, 2009, p142). He believed that language and its uses were fundamental to this, and that such an education could only be achieved by dialogue between the educators and the oppressed, illustrated in his argument that:

> *Authentic education is not carried on by 'A' for 'B' or by 'A' about 'B', but rather by 'A' with 'B', mediated by the world – a world which impresses and challenges both parties, giving rise to views or opinions about it. These views, impregnated with anxieties, doubts, hopes, or hopelessness, imply significant themes on the basis of which the program content of education can be built*

(Freire, 1970, p74)

Because Freire's work, and that of those who are influenced by him, such as Michael Apple or Henry Giroux, is focused on addressing issues of oppression and social injustice, it may be viewed as an educational approach which is inclusive of all, although to achieve the 'authentic' pedagogy Freire describes, all teachers would need to be politically aware, and critically conscious of the lives and experiences of their students. However, his pedagogy is not compatible with contemporary government policy which emphasises the 'delivery' of a centrally controlled curriculum. Despite this, many academics currently writing about Lifelong Learning are influenced by ideas around critical pedagogy and many teachers in the sector tend to lean naturally towards a Freirean approach. This can leave those teachers performing a balancing act between the approaches they believe are right for their students and those which are required by a constrained curriculum or by local and national policy, and illustrates the importance of thinking critically about the pedagogical approaches you use and being able to justify them in terms of authoritative literature.

This centrally controlled approach to education has given rise to a number of different approaches in recent years which have either become discredited or which have little basis in theory. For example, it has led to outcome-based forms of assessment which have profound implications for the way in which teachers teach and which have been criticised by Avis (2007, p161) as being *out of kilter with the needs of a knowledge economy*.

Other approaches, like personalisation, have found their way into policy (DfES, 2005) while others, such as learning styles, have been promoted by OFSTED, the quasi-independent inspection quango. Other approaches and initiatives which have given rise to criticism include activities based on notions of *emotional intelligence* (Goleman, 1995) and the *therapeutic* approach to education found in the sector (Ecclestone, 2004). In common with centrally controlled, outcome-based assessments, these approaches and initiatives have profoundly influenced pedagogy in FE colleges.

Pedagogic approaches

There is a wide-ranging and contested literature addressing issues of well-being in FE, much of which has its roots in notions of self-esteem, emotional literacy and personalisation. These are all recent concepts, which have found their way into the discourse (language) of both practitioners and policy makers. However, as recently as 1995, Rees discussed Post-Compulsory Education and Training (PCET) students with emotional and behavioural difficulties as having problems *not generally recognised* within the FE system. The increasing recognition of such difficulties, and the development of strategies to address them, has resulted in a focus within the sector on self-esteem. This has been reflected in work by Preston and Hammond (2003, p8) who found that over 90 per cent of respondents considered that *improved self esteem* was the most important wider benefit of FE, and in a 2005 paper by Ecclestone and McGiveney who questioned whether adult educators had become *obsessed with self esteem*.

Many of the initiatives used in the sector to promote self-esteem are related to the concept of emotional intelligence which was first proposed by Salovey and Mayer in 1990. Drawing on concepts and understandings of intelligence and of social intelligence, and earlier work including that of Gardner (1983) and of Thorndike in the 1920s, they proposed a framework for emotional intelligence which was a set of skills hypothesised to contribute to the accurate appraisal and expression of emotion in oneself and in others, and the use of feelings to motivate, plan and achieve in one's life. The emphasis of this paper, however, was not the role of emotional intelligence in education, but in the field of mental health. The concept was developed by Goleman in his own work in the field of business, though also related to issues of behaviour in schools (rather than colleges) and is marketed as practitioner/populist writing (for example, see Goleman, 1995 and 1998). He contributes to a defence of his work in a paper by Cherniss et al (2006) written in response to criticisms by Waterhouse (2006). Waterhouse critiqued the Mozart effect theory and multiple intelligence theory as well as the emotional intelligence theory and concluded that there was inadequate empirical support for these concepts and that *they should not be used as the basis for educational practice.* The concept has also been criticised by Mayer, one of its early proponents, who with Cobb (2000) argued that educational policy in this area has outpaced the science on which it is ostensibly based.

Similarly, the political concept of 'personalisation' was recently introduced to FE as part of broader government initiatives. Advocated by Leadbetter (2004) across all public services in a DEMOS (independent think-tank) publication, it has been rapidly introduced in the LLS and is concerned with providing a 'personalised' educational experience and learning plan for each individual. Despite now being well embedded in practice in the sector, it has, like the initiatives related to emotional literacy, been open to criticism: Ecclestone (2007) argues that policy discourse around well-being and personalisation resonates with images of the *diminished self*. Hartley (2007, p630) describes the concept of personalisation as *inchoate and incoherent* and argues that the government draws upon concepts of consumerism and marketing theory, rather than the Humanism and Romanticism more usually associated with education, in its justification of the concept.

Learning styles questionnaires, until recently also used as a matter of course across the sector, have also been subject to criticism. Learning styles theory owes much to the work of Kolb (for example, 1999) and to Honey and Mumford (1992) although there is an extensive body of literature on the subject and many different forms of learning styles questionnaires. The theory suggests that by analysing and diagnosing an individual's preferred way of learning, their learning experience can be tailored (or personalised) to suit that need and they will, as a consequence, achieve better outcomes. However, research on learning styles suggests that individual styles may change over time, and it could also be argued that it is in an individual's interests to acquire new and different strategies for learning. Further, a major study conducted by Coffield et al (2004) found that many questionnaires were of little or no value. They also criticised the research on which much learning styles theory is based, arguing that it tended to be drawn from diverse fields (such as business, education or psychology) and to focus on small-scale studies. Further, they argued that in much of the literature *the socio-economic and the cultural context of students' lives and of the institutions where they seek to learn tend to be omitted* (p142).

Despite the lack of empirical evidence supporting concepts such as learning styles, personalisation and emotional intelligence, they have produced a plethora of initiatives and activities across the sector and have been associated with an emerging 'therapeutic culture' in education. A therapeutic culture, or ethos, is one which assumes a deficit model of the student, in other words one based on the assumption that students have needs or problems which require intervention by the teacher or the institution. This culture has been criticised on philosophical grounds by, among others, Cigman (2004) and Kristjansson (2007). Ecclestone (2004 and 2007) has raised concerns that a therapeutic culture is leading to a *diminished self* who is ultimately disempowered in a manner inconsistent with social justice. However, the therapeutic approach has been defended by Hyland (2006, p299) who, while writing with specific reference to VET policy and practice in the UK, suggests that *an attention to the important values dimension of learning in the field does involve a therapeutic dimension of some kind*.

The implementation of approaches such as those described above is intended to support and promote the inclusion of all individuals, particularly the most disadvantaged and excluded in society, in education. However, a key issue with each is that they regard the student in deficit terms – as a person in need of help, support or some other kind of repair – rather than as individuals with valuable life experiences who have as much to teach us as we have to teach them. Regarding students as deficient in this way can also make us guilty of seeing them not as individuals, but as a homogeneous group determined by the characteristics they share, whether these are related to gender, race, disability, class, educational achievement or any other exclusionary characteristic. There is, therefore, a debate around the extent to which such initiatives as those described in this last section of the paper actively empower or disempower individuals. This is an important point for all of us to consider in the context of the values we hold about education.

Conclusion

This chapter has considered what might constitute a second chance education, and what the implications of that might be for the individual. It has also discussed some of the pedagogical approaches currently in use in the sector which are thereby associated with a second chance education. It has discussed some of the criticisms of second chance education and its associated pedagogies. It is important to remember that these criticisms are not personal criticisms of colleges, teachers or students, but of the educational structures and systems which control the nature of the curriculum teachers have to work with and the way in which they are required to teach it. These structures and systems also mean that different groups of learners are offered different types of curriculum, with very different work and life outcomes, in institutions which are held in different levels of esteem. It is also important to remember that the real value of a second chance education lies, perhaps, in its personal value to the individual in terms of achievement and the development of identity. This cannot be underestimated and can be, on occasion, transformational. As teachers, it is part of our responsibility to maximise those opportunities for transformation for all our students.

References

Ainley, P and Bailey, B (1997) *The business of learning: staff and student experiences of further education in the 1990s*. London: Cassell.

Atkins, L (2009) *Invisible students, impossible dreams: experiencing vocational education 14–19*. Stoke on Trent: Trentham Books.

Avis, J (2007) *Education, policy and social justice: learning and skills*. London: Continuum.

Bailey, B (2002) Further education in Aldrich, R (ed) *A century of education*. London: Routledge-Falmer.

Ball, SJ, Maguire, M, and Macrae, S (2000) *Choice, pathways and transitions post-16 new youth, new economies in the global city*. London: RoutledgeFalmer.

Bathmaker, A-M (2001) 'It's the perfect education': lifelong learning and the experience of foundation-level GNVQ students. *Journal of Vocational Education and Training* 53(1): 81–100.

Bathmaker, A-M (2005) Hanging in or shaping a future: defining a role for vocationally related learning in a 'knowledge' society. *Journal of Education Policy*, 20(1): 81–100.

Bathmaker, A-M (2006) Alternative futures: professional identity formation in English further education, in J Satterthwaite, W Martin and L Roberts (eds) *Discourse, resistance and identity formation*. Stoke on Trent: Trentham Books.

Bathmaker, A-M and Avis, J (2005) Becoming a lecturer in further education in England: the construction of professional identity and the role of communities of practice. *Journal of Education for Teaching*, 31(1): 47–62.

Bloomer, M (1998) 'They tell you what to do and then they let you get on with it': the illusion of progressivism in GNVQ. *Journal of Education and Work*, (11)2: 167–86.

Bloomer, M and Hodkinson, P (2000) Learning careers: continuity and change in young people's dispositions to learning. *British Educational Research Journal*, 26(5): 583–97.

Cherniss, C, Extein, M, Goleman, D and Weissberg, R (2006) Emotional intelligence: what does the research really indicate? *Educational Psychologist*, 41(4): 239–45.

Cigman, R. (2004) Situated self-esteem. *Journal of Philosophy of Education*, 38(1): 91–105.

Coffield, F, Moseley, D, Hall, E and Ecclestone, K (2004) *Learning styles and pedagogy in post-16 learning: a critical review*. London: LSRN.

Colley, H, James, D, Tedder, M and Diment, K (2003) Learning as becoming in vocational education and training: class, gender and the role of vocational habitus. *Journal of Vocational Education and Training*, 55(4): 471–97.

Colley, H, Mazzei, L and Lewin, C (2008) *The impact of 14–19 reforms on the career guidance profession: a disrupted community of practice*. Paper presented to the Annual Conference of the British Educational Research Association, Heriot-Watt University (5 September 2008).

Crossan, B, Field, J, Gallacher, J and Merrill, B (2003) Understanding participation in learning for non-traditional adult learners: learning careers and the construction of learning identities. *British Journal of Sociology of Education*, 24(1): 55–67.

DfES (2005) *14–19 education and skills*. London: Department for Education and Skills.

Ecclestone, K (2004) Learning or Therapy? The Demoralisation of Education. *British Journal of Educational Studies*, 52(2) 112–37.

Ecclestone, K (2007) Resisting images of the 'diminished self': the implications of emotional well-being and emotional engagement in education policy. *Journal of Education Policy*, 22(4): 455–70.

Ecclestone, K and McGiveney, V (2005) Are adult educators obsessed with developing self-esteem? *Adults Learning*, 16(5): 11–14.

Esland, G (1996) Education, training and nation state capitalism: Britain's failing strategy, in Avis, J, Bloomer, M, Esland, G, Gleeson, D and Hodkinson, P *Knowledge and nationhood education, politics and work.* London: Cassell.

Flinders, D and Thornton, S (2009) (eds) *The curriculum studies reader* (3rd edn). London: Routledge.

Freire, P (1970) *Pedagogy of the oppressed*. London: Penguin.

Gardner, H (1983) *Frames of mind: the theory of multiple intelligences*. New York: Basic Books.

Goleman, D (1995. *Emotional intelligence* New York: Bantam Books.

Goleman, D (1998) *Working with emotional intelligence* New York: Bantam Books.

Griffiths M (1998) *Educational research for social justice: getting off the fence*. Buckingham: Open University Press.

Griffiths, M (2003) *Action research for social justice in education: fairly different.* Buckingham: Open University Press.

Hartley, D (2007) Personalisation: the emerging 'revised' code of education? *Oxford Review of Education*, 33)(5): 629–42.

Hodkinson, P (1996) Careership: the individual, choices and markets in the transition to work, in Avis, J, Bloomer, M, Esland, G, Gleeson, D and Hodkinson, P *Knowledge and nationhood education, politics and work*. London: Cassell.

Hodkinson P and Bloomer M (2001) Dropping out of further education: complex causes and simplistic policy assumptions. *Research Papers in Education*, 16(2), 117–40(24).

Hodkinson, P, Sparkes, A and Hodkinson, H (1996) *Triumphs and tears: young people, markets and the transition from school to work*. London: David Fulton.

Hodkinson, P, Sparkes, A and Hodkinson, H (2007) Learning cultures in further education. *Educational Review*, 59(4): 399–413.

Hoelscher, M and Hayward, G (2008) *'Degrees of success' – working paper 3: analysing access to HE for students with different educational backgrounds: preliminary descriptive results*. Available: **www.tlrp.org/project%20sites/degrees/documents/Working_Paper_3_MH_GH_final2.doc** (Accessed November 2009).

Honey P and Mumford, A (1992) *The manual of learning styles*. Maidenhead: Peter Honey Publications.

Hyland, T (2006) Vocational education and training and the therapeutic turn. *Educational Studies*, 32(3): 299–306.

Knowles, M and associates (1984) *Andragogy in action: applying modern principles of adult education*. San Francisco: Jossey Bass.

Kolb, DA (1999) *The Kolb learning style inventory, version 3*. Boston, MA: Hay Group.

Kristjansson, K (2007) Justified self-esteem. *Journal of Philosophy of Education*, 41(2): 247–62.

Leadbetter, C (2004) *Personalisation through participation: a new script for public services 2004.* London: DEMOS.

LLUK (2006) *New overarching professional standards for teachers, tutors and trainers in the Lifelong Learning sector*. London: LLUK.

Macrae, S, Maguire, M and Ball, SJ (1997) Whose 'learning' society? A tentative deconstruction. *Journal of Education Policy*, 12(6): 499–509.

Mayer, J and Cobb, C (2000) Educational policy on emotional intelligence: does it make sense? *Educational Psychology Review*, 12(2): 163–83.

Oxford English Dictionary (2nd edn) (2003) Oxford: Oxford University Press.

Preston J and Hammond, C (2003) 'Practitioner views on the wider benefits of further education. *Journal of Further and Higher Education*, 27(2): 211–22.

Randle, K and Brady, N (1997a) Managerialism and professionalism in the 'Cinderella service'. *Journal of Vocational Education & Training*, 49(1): 121–39.

Randle, K and Brady, N (1997b) Further education and the new managerialism. *Journal of Further and Higher Education*, 21(2): 229–39.

Rees, S (1995) Students with emotional and behavioural difficulties: coping with a growing tide. *Journal of Further and Higher Education*, 19(2): 93–7.

Ross, S and Gray, J (2005) Transitions and re-engagement through second chance education. *The Australian Educational Researcher*, 32(3): 103–40.

Salovey, P and Mayer, JD (1990) Emotional intelligence. *Imagination, cognition, and personality,* 9: 185–211.

Smith, M (1996; 1999) Andragogy. *The encyclopaedia of informal education.*
  Available: **www.infed.org/lifelonglearning/b-andra.htm** (accessed November 2009).

Waterhouse, L (2006) Multiple intelligences, the Mozart effect, and emotional intelligence: a critical review. *Educational Psychologist,* 41(4): 207–25.

Professional skills for reading and writing

This section aims to support skills in reading widely, and in referencing and citation.

1 Using relevant literature effectively

This paper uses a wide range of literature, presenting often opposing arguments, and much of it is written in the style of a literature review. It is more supportive of some arguments than others. In other words, it is presenting, over all, the argument of the writer. The difference between an argument and *polemic* is that an argument will be supported by reference to relevant literature, as this is here. This does not necessarily mean that the argument is not controversial – many of the themes covered in this chapter are controversial. This makes it even more important that discussion of them is appropriately structured and supported. Remember, it is not important how *many* citations you use (students often ask how many they should put in an essay) but the *relevance* of the citations and the way in which they contribute to your argument *are* important.

2 Citation

Look at the number of citations in the chapter, and then count the number of direct quotes. An argument can 'flow' much more coherently if work is cited using paraphrasing or very brief quotes rather than multiple extended quotations. When referring to literature, it is not appropriate to summarise a whole paper or section. You should use the parts which are immediately relevant to the point under discussion, while reading the whole paper/chapter to ensure that your interpretation of the work is accurate (one of the authors cited in this chapter once read some work of mine and left an annotation which said 'this is NOT what I meant!'). This sentence or paragraph may be the only part of a book or paper which is relevant to your argument. Alternatively, different parts of a paper may be relevant to a wider discussion, in which case you would use them separately. For instance, count the number of times Bathmaker's 2001 paper has been cited in this chapter.

3 Currency of literature

In general, the work in papers is more current than books – the research on which an academic book is based can be as much as five years old by the time it is published. Contemporary work reflects current thinking, but that has often been influenced by older work which may be relevant to your essay. For example, many of the authors cited in this chapter who write about vocational education refer to work published in the 1980s when the new vocationalism first developed. However, they will also refer to more recent work at the same time. Again, relevance is what is most important.

Discussion

These tasks are to help you develop your understanding of the concepts and arguments in this chapter. The tasks involve critical reflection on the concepts and arguments, and the development of counter arguments. This will help you to structure written discussions considering opposing or differing points of view.

DISCUSSION TASK

Draw a line forming a continuum between Freire's notions of a pedagogy of the oppressed and a circumscribed curriculum delivered to centralised requirements (such as an NVQ credential taught according to pre-set schemes of work with pre-set assessments). Where would you place your own teaching on this continuum? Why? Where would you like to be? Where would your students like to be?

DISCUSSION TASK

Choose one of the points or arguments made in this chapter and make notes to create an opposing, or different interpretation. To help with this, you should look up some of the references used and see if your interpretation of the original work is the same as mine.

DISCUSSION TASK

As you read, critique the chapter. Consider the arguments made and the evidence provided in support of those arguments. Were the arguments reasoned and well justified? Was adequate evidence provided in support of the arguments? How might it have been structured differently?

FURTHER READING FURTHER READING FURTHER READING FURTHER READING

Avis, J and Bathmaker, A (2004) Critical pedagogy, performativity and a politics of hope: trainee further education lecturer practice. *Research in Post-Compulsory Education*, 9(2): 301–16.

Ecclestone, K and Hayes, D (2008) *The dangerous rise of therapeutic education.* London: Routledge.

Freire, P (2004) *The pedagogy of hope*. London: Continuum.

5

Responding to learners' numeracy and literacy needs

The aims of this chapter are to provide:

- a contextual framework of the national issues relating to numeracy and literacy;
- a review of successive government responses designed to address concerns with numeracy and literacy skills;
- an indication of the impact of these policies on the FE sector.

What to look for

- From your reading consider the differences and parallels in government responses between the different education sectors.
- From your experience compare how policy statements have been interpreted in practice in *your* workplace (which initiatives, if any, do you believe apply to you?).

Author details

Before taking up her current post lecturing in the Lifelong Learning Department at Nottingham Trent University, Sheine Peart worked in FE for 15 years, teaching numeracy, communication, basic and key skills to learners on a wide variety of vocational and academic programmes at different levels.

Responding to learners' numeracy and literacy needs

Sheine Peart

Abstract

There is ongoing and wide-ranging debate regarding learners' numeracy and literacy levels and needs. Good numeracy and literacy skills are fundamental to successfully accessing the curriculum and are required for all types of employment. The government, committed to raising the skills level of the nation, have over successive years, made improving numeracy and literacy standards a central part of national education policies. This paper aims to provide a contextual framework for these initiatives and to track governmental response in addressing the UK's low skills level. It explores the professional responsibilities now placed upon tutors because of this situation and considers some of the strategies that have been suggested to address this need.

Introduction – a national context

The most effective ways to teach children, young people and adults to become literate and numerate, and enable them to apply this information in learning environments and beyond, have been a focus of discussion and research by academics and education professionals for many years. However, it is not only academics and educationalists who are interested in this question; indeed, in recent years it has become an issue of national importance.

In 1999, Moser reported that:

> *something like one adult in five in this country is not functionally literate and far more people have problems with numeracy. This is a shocking situation and a sad reflection on past decades of schooling. It is one of the reasons for relatively low productivity in our economy and it cramps the lives of millions of people.*
>
> (Moser, 1999, p8)

The extent of this problem becomes even more apparent if skills levels in the UK are compared to other western economies, as Table 5.1 clearly illustrates.

Table 5.1: Percentage of adults with low literacy and numeracy skills in 1997

	Literacy	Numeracy
Britain	23	23
United States	22	21
New Zealand	20	20
Canada	17	17
Australia	17	17
Germany	12	7
Sweden	7	7

(Moser, 1999, pp17–18)

In 2006 Leitch reiterated Moser's findings, indicating that *almost 17 million adults have difficulty with number and 5 million are not functionally literate* (p1). Furthermore, he iden-tified that the *UK skills base remains weak by international standards, holding back productivity, growth and social justice* (p3). Leitch also emphasised the link between skills and national prosperity suggesting good literacy and numeracy were fundamental to the *economic and social health of the UK* (p1). Significantly Leitch claimed that *continuing to improve our schools will not be enough to solve these problems [and] over 70 per cent of our 2020 workforce have already completed their compulsory education* (p1). It is against this national picture of low skills, the need to remain economically competitive, having to address decades of previous low achievement and the recognition that improving achieve-ment in schools alone is not sufficient to solve these significant problems, that FE has been implicitly charged with addressing this skills deficit, in the same way that it has taken responsibility for addressing other national skills shortages.

The impact of such a low skills base, Moser suggested, is twofold: firstly, it hinders growth and economic prosperity, and secondly, because so many social interactions are dependent on individuals having certain fundamental knowledge and understanding, low skills cause social exclusion for families and individuals, making it difficult for them to find and retain employment or to join in a variety of recreational activities. These two key themes of national economic well-being and social inclusion have been further developed and reappear in later government reports including the 1996 Tomlinson Report on Inclusion; the 2002 Success for All Strategy; and the 2005 *Education and Skills* White Paper.

Although often grouped together, and described alternatively as core, basic, key, essential and life skills, literacy and numeracy present different challenges to learners and tutors. Some of these issues have been created by common perceptions of the two areas and widely held beliefs of the complexity of the subjects. In this regard literacy enjoys a much more favourable position than numeracy, and while it is accepted that there are significant numbers of adults with literacy problems (as demonstrated by Moser, 1999, and Leitch, 2006), most people in the UK can read and write to some degree and virtually all people have developed skills in speaking and listening. In contrast, numeracy has a far less positive image and is often presented as a *demanding subject, in which only exceptionally intelligent people can actually succeed* (Nardi and Steward, 2003, p357). Whereas many learners may be willing to try to develop their literacy skills, some learners have completely disengaged from numeracy and now form part of a group which openly displays a *bias against maths* (Kowson, 2004), which prevents them from participating and even attempting to improve their skills. This differential response to the two subject areas is partly responsible for creating the 'spiky profiles' of achievement shown by many learners.

The issue relating to achievement in these key areas is further complicated by gender differences. In the past girls have performed, and continue to perform, particularly well in the Arts subjects. Their linguistic skills develop sooner and are more advanced than those of their male counterparts. This created a division where girls performed well in languages and humanities but lagged behind their male colleagues in maths and sciences. In part this difference was attributed to a discriminatory curriculum where *girls were persuaded, subtly and openly, that traditionally masculine subjects such as the 'hard' sciences and maths were 'not for them'* (Francis, 2000, p5). However, in recent years this situation, while not quite reversed, has significantly improved, and girls first matched, and then exceeded the achievement of boys in GSCE maths (Brettingham, 2007).

These complex and interlinked circumstances have over time produced a situation where it is estimated *26 million people of working age have levels of literacy and numeracy below those expected of school leavers* (National Audit Office 2004, p1). This cycle of repeated and continuing low achievement has combined to hinder economic growth, and, during economic downturns, threatens to challenge recovery by producing a skills shortage. The lack of an appropriately skilled adult population competent in literacy and numeracy at the required level is no longer an individual concern, but has become elevated to an issue of national importance.

Government responses to developing numeracy and literacy skills

Some researchers have suggested that many students *may well have been disenchanted by inappropriate lessons, which do not stimulate learners* (Noble and Bradford, 2000, p101). Consequently, some learners have chosen to dissociate from all subjects including literacy and numeracy and have become part of an anti-learning culture which has contributed to low achievement and the skills shortage now apparent in the UK. The government, aware of and concerned by this difficulty, has responded in a number of different ways.

In 1996, the government launched the National Literacy and Numeracy Strategy for primary schools, where a separate hour for language skill development was set aside, and a second hour for numeracy development took place every day. This strategy was based on the simple idea that if improvements were to be made, there needed to be structural changes to the system which would ensure that *all* learners were provided with an opportunity to develop appropriate skills early in their educational career. This was reinforced with the high profile 'Back to Basics' campaign in 1998, when the then Education Secretary, David Blunkett, stated in a press campaign that *literacy and numeracy have too often been subsumed into other subjects. It is no surprise that so many pupils leave primary school ill-equipped in the three-Rs* (Blunkett, 1998). Although not openly articulated, there was an implicit suggestion that many teachers had been in some way negligent, careless or incompetent and had failed to provide adequate tuition to young people which would ensure that by the time they left primary school they were both literate and numerate.

To address this problem a clear, centrally designed structure was needed which would compensate for the deficits of the past. This was achieved by introducing a framework for teaching literacy and numeracy in all schools which was designed to give all pupils the chance to develop the essential skills they needed. In tangent with the primary framework, a similar initiative to raise standards was also introduced for Key Stage 3 in secondary schools. Although in no way a response to the problems of the adult population, this strategy at least indicated that the government had recognised that a long-term solution was needed to tackle these concerns, which involved working with the very youngest learners who were just beginning their education. By introducing this strategy there was also a tacit recognition that it would take many years before the benefits of such a structured approach would work through the system and translate into positive benefits for adult learners.

However, it is interesting to reflect upon the level of status accorded to these achievement promoting initiatives. Although the government was aware that there were significant numbers of primary school children leaving schools without appropriate skills in literacy and numeracy, the framework for teaching only remained at 'recommended' status level. This meant that schools could, if they chose, not follow this framework. It could be argued this was a recognition of the professionalism of teachers: a recognition that they could be trusted to design a relevant and meaningful curriculum which would develop children's skills. However, because schools needed to present good reasons for *not* adopting this framework such an interpretation is unlikely.

By comparison, whereas the government took clear action for the statutory sector, changes in the post-compulsory sector to address the needs of adult learners took longer to be introduced and it was not until 2001 that a coherent national programme for adults became available with the launch of the national Skills for Life (SfL) strategy. Like the primary strategy, this strategy was designed to improve the skills level of its target audience by improving the quality and consistency of provision – this time in colleges. However, unlike the primary or secondary sector, FE colleges were not placed under the same pressure to adopt the adult literacy or numeracy core curricula. In practice though, many colleges chose to use the frameworks produced by the basic skills agency (BSA), and welcomed a standardised unified approach to guide and inform their curriculum planning. The purpose of these new curricula was threefold. Firstly, they were intended to specify the entitlement for all adults needing numeracy and literacy tuition; secondly, they described the content of taught programmes and thirdly, they were designed to assist teachers in planning to meet the individual needs of their students. In this way the government was able to exert some level of influence over literacy and numeracy teaching in colleges. The SfL strategy was followed in 2005 by the introduction of the National Standards in Adult Literacy, Numeracy and ICT. This differed from the adult basic skills curriculum, in that it purely indicated the levels of achievement expected of all adults and did not provide suggestions on how these skills should be taught or offer ideas on learning activities. These standards were to be achieved by all adult learners whether they continued to study at school, transferred to a college or undertook work-based training. The standards therefore applied to the maintained sector, the post-compulsory sector and employment. However, it is important to note that while the government was able to use its considerable power to determine what was taught in schools, and to a degree in colleges, this same level of influence did not extend to training in the workplace.

The SfL strategy has been significant in helping many adults develop their skills in literacy and numeracy and through this programme 750,000 low-skilled learners had taken part in courses to help improve their English and maths skills by 2004. Furthermore, it appears that the government is likely to achieve its 2010 target of engaging with an additional 1.5 million low-skilled learners (NAO, 2004). Although this may appear to be limited success in the context of the scale of the problem, as the government has made successive progress in reaching its targets, it is now encountering learners who are harder to engage with, many of whom consist of disenfranchised 'hard to reach' groups.

While the primary framework and the adult basic skills curriculum captured many learners and helped them to improve their skills, there remained a population of younger adults, often studying level 2 (GSCE grades A*–C and equivalent courses) and level 3 programmes (A levels and equivalent courses), who were not being effectively reached by either of these strategies. The government responded to this need by introducing its key skills strategy following recommendations in the 1996 Dearing Report. The key skills strategy was a suite of qualifications designed to run alongside existing programmes to enable learners to develop their skills in English, maths and other life skill areas. The key skills programme was intended to be practically based and to be embedded in real-life examples where learners could see the immediate relevance of needing good literacy and numeracy skills; and it led to a qualification designed to appeal to future employers. For those learners who were studying level 3 programmes, key skills qualifications also carried HE points, which would support applications to universities. The key skills programme was thus designed to have broad appeal, and would be attractive to learners, future employers and to colleges and universities.

However, the key skills initiative suffered an image and publicity problem from the day it was introduced. Principally available at levels 1, 2 and 3, (although also available at levels 4 and 5), key skills qualifications were in competition with an already existing suite of qualifications. At level 1 they were primarily in competition with basic skills qualifications; at level 2 they were pitched against GCSEs; and at level 3 they were matched against A levels. As the expected standard on leaving secondary education was to have GCSEs at C or above in maths and English (constituting a level 2 qualification), the population most likely to be studying key skills often perceived this alternative qualification as a 'consolation prize' intended for those who had not earlier attained the necessary level 2 standard. Colleges, keen to maximise their funding, would often encourage learners to study key skills. Learners enrolled on level 2 programmes, however, had little real choice here as their progression onto a level 3 course was often dependent on successfully completing level 2 key skills. Equally problematic was the fact that learners entered for key skills level 1 felt patronised or belittled, and similarly learners studying at level 3 were reluctant to complete key skills as they had already attained the necessary level 2 standard. The argument that key skills would confer university points was rarely accepted, as key skills qualifications were worth so few points that this would only make a difference to the most borderline candidates. Although the key skills programme was designed to have wide appeal, in reality, it appeared to be the epitome of a qualification designed by committee, and actually pleased very few.

Key skills are now to be replaced by functional skills qualifications as part of reforms to 14–19 education and *irrespective of the path a young person chooses, every student will be taught functional skills in maths, English and ICT from 2010* (DCSF, 2009, p6). However, whether or not functional skills will be a success, and how they will be received and perceived by learners, employers and universities, will only become apparent with the passage of time.

The impact on the FE sector

By the time learners enter the FE sector they are expected to have developed literacy and numeracy skills to level 2 standard. Achievement at this level would be demonstrated either by achieving a GCSE at grade C or above, or by passing the adult basic skills test at level 2. At this stage all learners should have developed literacy skills that allow them to:

- *listen and respond to spoken language;*
- *orally communicate straightforward and detailed information;*
- *engage in discussion with one or more people in different situations;*
- *read and understand a range of texts and communicate information in writing.*

(DfES, 2005, p19)

And in numeracy they are expected to show the ability to:

- *read and understand mathematical information;*
- *specify and describe a practical activity;*
- *generate results to an appropriate level of accuracy;*
- *present and explain results.*

(ibid)

However, not all learners entering the FE environment have been able to demonstrate these skills, and FE tutors often found they were working with learners whose skills were below this level. In this context all FE tutors were now expected to work with colleagues to ensure *the development of numeracy and literacy skills of learners* (LLUK, 2007, p2) to help learners achieve the required standard. In practical terms this meant FE tutors were obliged to:

- determine where there were opportunities for learners to develop their literacy and numeracy skills in all their programmes;
- teach literacy and numeracy skills identified within their courses;
- support learners in developing their skills so that they could achieve the national level 2 standard, if they had not already done so.

To achieve this, FE tutors were encouraged to use an embedded skills approach in teaching and to exploit literacy and numeracy opportunities wherever they occurred in their courses, regardless of whether or not they had been trained to teach these subjects. It is interesting to reflect that while this approach was discouraged in the statutory sector, and there was a greater emphasis on providing distinct learning opportunities via the literacy and numeracy hours, it has been and continues to be positively supported and encouraged in the post-compulsory sector. Such an approach is intended to ensure that learners develop competence in these skills and have the confidence and motivation to use their skills both at work and in life.

While *all* tutors now needed to assist learners in developing their literacy and numeracy skills, there has also been a considerable effort to raise the skills levels of specialist literacy and numeracy tutors. This initiative has been supported by the introduction of new qualifications in teaching literacy and numeracy at levels 4 and 5. In many ways, these qualifications have been positively welcomed by literacy and numeracy tutors, who have now been able to achieve higher level professional qualifications, and to shed the image of providing low-level courses to less able students.

By the time learners enter the FE environment they will have experienced a range of different approaches to teaching literacy and numeracy, from discrete autonomous models through to models which are fully embedded into the curriculum. And yet, for many learners these approaches have so far not been successful. If this curriculum engineering has been unsuccessful for some learners, then what strategy would be useful? The key here is motivation, as we only learn effectively *when we are motivated to do so* (Martin, Lovat and Purnell, 2007, p9). Perhaps the answer is that tutors need to work to increase student motivation so that they will be more willing to engage with learning. Wallace (2007) suggests that learners are more likely to be positively motivated to learn when they are clear on the intended purposes of activities; have good relationships with tutors; are able to make contributions to the session and when the tutor provides sufficient flexibility which recognises other external commitments learners may have. Within FE, it is not adequate to simply consider content and the structural features of learning, which is why merely promoting an embedded approach to learning could still be unsuccessful; but it is critical to remember learners' individuality and to work to accommodate this within the learning environment.

Conclusion

It is clear that the need to improve the numeracy and literacy skills of the adult population and young people has become an issue of major importance in recent times and the government has taken significant steps to address this issue. The impact of these initiatives has been wide ranging, and has influenced all sectors of education from primary through to post-compulsory education and into the workplace. Tutors have been expected to respond positively to these changes and, in addition to teaching vocational courses and other programmes, they are now tasked to support learners in developing their skills in literacy and numeracy. This has raised important issues for many tutors who have had to explore ways to include the integration of literacy and numeracy opportunities into their programmes, and for specialists in literacy and numeracy to undertake CPD by adding the newly introduced qualifications to their existing ones. The issue of the best model for developing learners' skills has not been confirmed and is likely to remain an ongoing issue for some time yet, and it is very likely further change can be expected.

References

Blunkett, D (1998) Press Release 13.01.98 **http://news.bbc.co.uk/I/hi/uk/46975.stm** (accessed January 2010).

Brettingham, M (2007) Gender gap yawns wider in schools. *Times Educational Supplement,* 6 July 2007, **www.tes.co.uk/article.aspx?storycode=2407113** (accessed January 2010).

DCSF (2009) *14–19 briefing: making change happen.* London: DCSF.

DfES (2005) *National standards for adult literacy, numeracy and ICT.* Norwich: QCA publications.

Francis, B (2000) *Boys, girls and achievement – addressing the classroom issues.* London: Routledge.

Kowson, J (2004) This innumerate isle. *Times Educational Supplement,* 17 September 2004, **www.tes.co.uk/article.aspx?storycode=2033102** (accessed January 2010).

Leitch, S (2006) *Prosperity for all in the global economy – world class skills.* London: HMSO.

LLUK (2007) *Addressing literacy, language, numeracy and ICT needs in education and training: defining the minimum core of teachers' knowledge, understanding and personal skills.* London: LLUK.

Martin, T, Lovat, C and Purnell, G (2007) *The really useful literacy book.* Abingdon: Routledge.

Moser, C (1999) *Improving literacy and numeracy: a fresh start.* London: DfEE.

Nardi, E and Steward, S (2003) Is mathematics T.I.R.E.D.? A profile of quiet disaffection in the secondary mathematics classroom. *British Educational Research Journal,* 29(3): 345–67.

National Audit Office (2004) *Skills for life: improving adult literacy and numeracy.* London: The Stationery Office.

Noble, C and Bradford, W (2000) *Getting it right for boys... and girls.* London: RoutledgeFalmer.

Wallace, S (2007) *Getting the buggers motivated in FE.* London: Continuum.

Professional skills for reading and writing

This section is designed to help you to extend your critical understanding of the paper you have just read. It challenges you to explore the issues raised within the context of your own practice and to develop your own arguments to respond to the key issues raised. It considers three principal themes:

1. chronologies of events;
2. the use of reference material;
3. the impact of personal experience.

1 Chronologies

Events in education texts and papers may not always be presented in chronological order. This is because policies often overlap and may be revised or amended over time. Furthermore, it would be rare for a single policy to apply to all sectors, although there could be cross-over between sectors. For example, while *Every Child Matters* legislation applies to nursery, primary and secondary education, it only applies to learners who are 18 years and younger in the FE sector and would not apply to the majority of learners in HE. In addition to this, often there is no specified end date to educational initiatives and they tend to continue, either intact or in part, until they are replaced by another initiative. This multi-layered web of policies and programmes can make it very difficult to understand what policies apply to which environments.

You may find it useful to re-read the section on government responses to developing numeracy and literacy skills. Try to produce a time line which indicates in chronological order when successive initiatives were introduced and to which sectors they applied. Are there any initiatives which appear to apply to more than one sector? From your own knowledge and understanding of wider issues, can you envisage any circumstances where it may be difficult to deliver these initiatives, for example in young offenders institutes or pupil referral units?

2 The use of referenced material

The article you have just read used referenced material from a number of different sources. This is common for many academic articles. Why would researchers choose to include the work of others in their writing? How has this material been used? What function does this serve? How does it influence your reading of the article? How do you use or how could you use sources in your own writing? Which sources would you be most likely to use? How would you make this choice?

3 The impact of personal experience

It can sometimes be difficult to retain a professional distance when writing about events in which you have been involved, and your personal views may influence how you present information. While it is acceptable to offer interpretations and to draw on your own working experience, it is important in academic writing to maintain a balanced view. In your view, then, has this article managed to maintain an academic and scholarly approach to the issues discussed or has the writer's personal experiences unduly influenced how this paper has been presented? What examples of balanced argument or personal bias can you locate in the article?

Discussion

The following discussion topic will assist you in developing an academic response to the issues raised in the paper you have just read. It will help you formulate your own ideas and enable you to challenge or support views that may be expressed in your own workplace.

DISCUSSION TASK

This paper set out the national framework and successive government responses to address literacy and numeracy concerns in the UK. It described how different institutions and different sectors were expected to support learners' development of literacy and numeracy. However, there can be a real or perceived difference between central government policy and local action. Consider the following questions in relation to your own workplace.

- Can you specifically identify how national policy has been implemented?
- In terms of a response time, how long was it before the initiative was adopted?
- Who was given responsibility for implementing this decision and how was this resourced?

Although you may not necessarily be able to influence how initiatives are carried out at work, it is always useful to have an awareness of the structures and machinery responsible for implementing policy initiatives. Such awareness will give you a feeling of greater control over your own working environment and will allow you to consider your own response to new initiatives.

FURTHER READING FURTHER READING **FURTHER READING** FURTHER READING

Much of the further reading related to developing literacy and numeracy skills will be from government briefing papers and documents. While this information will ensure that you keep up to date with current initiatives, it may be less helpful in supporting you on how to teach. To support you in this area you may find it useful to read the following journals:

Literacy Today
Mathematics in school

You may also find it helpful to consider the following book:

Appleyard, N and Appleyard, K (2009) *The minimum core for language and literacy: knowledge, understanding and personal skills.* Exeter: Learning Matters.
Peart, S (2009) *The minimum core for numeracy: knowledge, understanding and personal skills.* Exeter: Learning Matters.

6
Assessment 14–19

The aims of this chapter are to provide:

- an example of academic writing style;
- a template for structuring a piece of academic writing;
- a discussion of key issues in the assessment of 14–19 year olds;
- a review of the policy and legislation which has shaped assessment in the LLS;
- a consideration of the ways in which assessment theory is reflected in practice.

What to look for

- As you read, notice how the writer has structured this paper. How useful do you find the headings he has used in 'signposting' the focus of each section?
- Notice the use this writer has made of an appendix. For what reason do you think the material in the appendix has not simply been incorporated into the text?

Author details

Pete Bradshaw is a lecturer at The Open University who is researching student perspectives of assessment at 16. He works on a professional development programme for teachers in the area of technology and learning. He joined The Open University in 2009 from Nottingham Trent University where he lectured in Education with a particular interest in teacher education and research methods. He was the Standards and Quality Manager for the School of Education and, covering a secondment, acting team leader for Continuing Education, covering 14–19, CPD and Lifelong Learning. He has been a chief examiner for GNVQ and principal examiner for A levels. He has authored chapters of textbooks on GNVQ Information Technology and presented widely on e-learning and professional online communities.

Assessment 14–19

Pete Bradshaw

Abstract

Drawing on current theory and research, this chapter addresses questions both about how assessment is used (and sometimes over-used) in teaching 14–19, and whether current assessment practices, for example in subjects such as ICT, are fit for purpose. It introduces the reader to current theories and practices.

Introduction

It would seem fairly self-evident that the objective of education is for learning to have taken place. But how do we know we have learned something? As teachers, how do we know our students have learned something? How do we know learning is taking place? The answer to these fundamental questions lies in the domain of assessment. Assessment is the instrument by which we can determine the nature of what has been learned.

Is there a danger that, as with all instruments of 'measurement', the use of assessment affects what has been, or what is being, learned? Do we distort the learning process through the application of assessment processes? Such distortion may come from teachers who 'teach to the test' or from learners who focus their activity on what it is they will be assessed on rather than the wider learning that may be on offer in any course. Thus we have two key, and to some extent opposing, issues: the need to have a way of determining the extent of learning and the need to ensure that this is done without unduly distorting what is learned. We will address both of these issues together in the rest of this chapter. We start with an exploration of the theory and practice of assessment and follow this with a look at the policies that shape the way in which we assess.

What is assessment? Theory, research and practice

In the introduction we discuss the centrality of assessment to the business of learning and teaching. What does this look like in practice? Firstly, we need to consider two 'spaces' in which assessment takes place – assessment while teaching and learning is in progress, and assessment at the end of a period of teaching and learning. In technical terms, we refer to these as *formative* and *summative* assessment (see, for example, Stobart and Gipps, 1997).

While these two terms are intrinsically wrapped up in notions of time – formative assessment taking place during learning, summative assessment taking place after learning – they have other dimensions. Formative assessment carries with it the opportunity for altering the course of the learning. You may see this in the derivation of the term: future learning is *formed* by the assessment. Black and Wiliam (1998) deepened this relationship through the development of their formulation of assessment for learning. Here, they postulate, assessment is carried out primarily to inform and direct future learning. The purpose of the assessment is *for learning* rather than *for assessment*. As we teach we are assessing. As we learn, or as our students learn, they are assessing. The process is continuous but can also be marked by specific opportunities to bring the assessment to the forefront. Assessment here is both an implicit and an explicit activity.

This is contrasted by *assessment* of *learning* which is, by definition, summative and an end in itself. It could be argued, however, that even in this case the results of the assessment affect the future learning paths – whether that be in terms of opening up or closing down options for progression or, more subtly, giving feedback to learners (and teachers) about strengths and weaknesses.

While assessment is explicitly addressed by one domain (Domain E: Assessment for Learning) in the Professional Standards, its more continuous nature is reflected in several of the other domains (see Appendix on pages 61–63). In Domain A we see that teachers are required to value the *progress and development* of learners. Domain B includes the need for *communicating effectively and appropriately with learners to enhance learning*. Domain D includes a commitment to *learner participation in the planning of learning* and planning to *meet the aims and needs of individual learners* to gather and use *learner feedback* and to *negotiate and record appropriate learning goals and strategies with learners* (LLUK, 2007).

How do these statements help us define the scope of assessment? We can see that assessment includes the evaluation of learning, and of teaching, and involves learners in the process through negotiation of goals. Once such goals are determined, a framework is in place against which assessment may be made. Such a framework also provides us with a model for discussing assessment in theory and practice. The activities and processes of assessment must be planned and designed. These are then put into use with the involvement of learners. Finally, they produce 'results' that inform future learning and give feedback on progress and on the effectiveness of the teaching. Each of these stages will now be considered in turn.

Designing assessment

In the previous section we discussed ideas of formative and summative assessment. These define the *type* of assessment to some extent, but are more concerned with *purpose.* The reason for carrying out the activity defines its type and influences its design. If, for example, an activity is designed as formative then there needs to be opportunity for feedback to learners as to what they need to do next. The assessment here feeds into future learning. It may be worth restating that while all formative assessment will have this 'assessment for learning' aspect, summative assessment may also have developmental outputs.

What other types of, and purposes for, assessment can we identify? Intrinsic to most assessment is the idea of criteria. If we are to measure learning – what are the criteria that we are using to measure? Such criterion referenced assessment provides for some form of objective judgement. The learning, or rather its manifestation, is judged against some statements or benchmarks. As the judgement is against criteria, the grading of the performance of a student is not affected by the performance of others. Alternatives to criteria referencing are norm referencing and ipsative assessment. In the former, usually applied to summative assessments, categorisation is made according to the same normal distribution of performance. Thus it might be that 15 per cent of students get a particular grade. Norm referencing means that this percentage is maintained and criteria are adjusted to allow for such maintenance. Marks are allocated according to a predetermined distribution. Here a student's mark is determined not only by performance, but by how that performance compares with the rest of the cohort.

Ipsative assessment provides for measurement relative to a student's own previous performance. Application of such assessment, independent of objective criteria, may be seen in sports with the notion of 'personal best' or in situations where 'value-added' or 'progress' measures are deemed to be more important than absolute measures. Such ipsative assessment requires the setting down of initial or benchmark measures. Initial assessment of this type is not restricted to such uses, however. More commonly it provides initial diagnosis of student capability or aptitude prior to commencement of a course. This may be coupled with the setting of initial learning goals and targets.

Once the overall type and timing of assessment is decided on, there is then the choice of assessment methods to be used. While this choice is linked to the purpose, it is also influenced by the type of learning to be assessed. Where, for example, this is primarily concerned with knowledge, the assessment may, perhaps, be in the form of an examination or test. Where the judgement is of a learner's ability to apply the knowledge or to test understanding then other methods may be more appropriate – assignment, presentation, interview, observation.

A key question in the design of any assessment is the extent to which it is 'fair'. Indeed the Professional Standards make this explicit; for example, in ES2: *Teachers are committed to assessing the work of learners in a fair and equitable manner* (see Appendix on page 62). But what do we mean by 'fair' and is this open to different individual interpretations? We will now look at issues of fairness and how we can take steps to ensure that any assessment is robust.

Crucial to issues of fairness and equitability in assessment are the concepts of validity, reliability and sufficiency (see, for example, Stobart and Gipps, 1997; Black and Wiliam, 2006; Stobart, 2006). Of these, validity is probably the one over which there is the most debate. What is meant by a valid assessment? Crucially it is one which assesses what it purports to assess. This is technically known as construct validity. There are ways of analysing assessments to check that this is the case but, in themselves, these do not guarantee that an assessment is 'fair'.

In all learning situations, but especially in 14–19 and beyond, the notion of authenticity is also important. The definition of validity would then be extended to be assessment which measures what it purports to measure in an authentic way. Questions to ask would be: Is the assessment method appropriate to the nature of the course and the students? Do the tasks represent the learning and context authentically or are they contrived for the sake of assessment (Goodwin, 1997; Tombari and Borich, 1999)? There are often issues of authenticity when technology is concerned. It may be that the assessment task to assess capability with technology is one step removed from the capability itself. For example, are we trying to assess students' ability to use a piece of software by asking them to write about it, or produce a portfolio about it, when we should be observing their use of it? Assessment method is central to authenticity and hence to validity. On the other hand, it might be that we are using technology to assess understanding and skills in a subject domain for which the technology is not the most appropriate medium. Often this is done in the name of flexibility and student choice, but maybe making students sit an assessment on a computer is less authentic than a scheduled presentation, observation or workplace demonstration of their capability.

Once a valid assessment is designed the next question is to ask how reliable it is. Reliability here means how well the assessment might be replicated and how independent it is of factors beyond those which are being assessed. The issues of technology discussed above come into play again here. It might also be that an assessment method is better suited to some students than others (perhaps for demographic or cultural reasons), or that assessment is too dependent on subjective interpretation by the assessor. Thus students who might have the same capability achieve different results because of these extrinsic factors.

The final issue is that of sufficiency. This may be explained by asking the question, 'Have we enough assessment activities to be sure that our results are reliable and valid?' Equally important is to be careful not to have too much assessment. The danger is one that was related earlier. Students are focused on what they need to do for assessment. If there is too much to do then the course becomes subverted by this focus.

New College Nottingham
Learning Centres

Validity and reliability can be enhanced by processes of moderation and peer review. Moderation is traditionally limited to checking marked work to look for agreements and differences. Along with peer review, however, it can also be applied to the design phase of assessment to get consensus on whether the tasks set allow for validity and reliability, whether they are authentic and whether they are sufficient. A simple check would be to look at the learning outcomes for any course and to map where they are assessed (Biggs, 1999). Where possible this can be complemented by student involvement in the assessment and target-setting process. This is the subject of the next section.

Learner involvement

It may be argued that assessment is traditionally something that is 'done' to learners. Students take examinations, write coursework, sit online tests. The move from assessment *of* learning towards assessment *for* learning requires a concomitant shift in the locus of authority when assessment judgements are being made. Rather than the remote 'examiner', the assessor is someone with whom the learner is in contact and has a dialogue. It may even be that the learner self assesses or is involved in peer assessment.

These notions of learner involvement are explicit in the Professional Standards, and may be clearly seen in ES3 (see Appendix on pages 61–63). Furthermore, the principles of learner engagement in, and with, the assessment process resonates with the values and commitments expected elsewhere in the Professional Standards. How better to demonstrate the valuing of learners and understanding of their motivations than to make the assessment process as participative as possible, gaining feedback from students as well as providing it?

Historically students who have 'been done to' by assessment have only been able to take an active part in the process after the event – for example in appeals procedures. Clearly though, this involvement can begin at the point of initial assessment through a dialogue with those administering the diagnostic. It can continue through negotiated target-setting and reflection on progress, can encompass self- and peer review and can be embodied in the making of the assessment activities as transparent as possible. This last point means avoiding assessments that 'ambush' the learner by imposing unexpected tests.

But with transparency comes a danger of losing reliability. Does the closer relationship between learner and assessor provide room for loss of objectivity? Perhaps so, but in most cases this can be countered by robust moderation processes. Learner involvement always requires discussion in some form. At the heart of this is feedback, which is the subject of the next section.

Feedback

Feedback can be given to students in a number of ways (LSIS, 2005). Assessors may organise tutorials or give annotated comments on work as formative assessment. In peer review students will review each other's work – perhaps with template evaluation sheets to report on the key points or learning objectives. However this is done, the progress a learner has made must be established and goals for future development and learning identified (Black and Wiliam, 1998; Black et al, 2003). It may be that such goal-setting is done after a series of assessments rather than after each one. For example, peer review may be combined with negotiations with a tutor. Nevertheless, the relationship between feedback and progress is clear and needs to be made explicit to the student.

The Professional Standards, while addressing feedback to the learner in aspects of learner involvement (for example, ES3) and values (for example, AP1.1), also exemplify another aspect to feedback (see Appendix on pages 61–63). That is the feedback that a teacher gets from assessment about his or her *own* performance. James and Pedder (2006) put teacher learning at the heart of effective student learning. For us, as teachers, to become truly reflective practitioners we need to have evidence about the effectiveness of our practice from as wide a range of sources as possible. The data provided by assessment is a rich source for this, but caution is needed as the assessment task may well be set by the same person who carries out the assessment, thus making it possible that there may be a lack of objectivity and a skewing of data. With careful use of such evidence, however, we change as teachers. Indeed, *implementing assessment for learning requires personal change* (Black et al, 2003, p80).

Why do we assess the way we do? Policy and standards

In the preceding sections of this paper we have discussed the ways in which assessment activities are designed and how learners may be involved in the process of assessment. But what are the external drivers on teachers and institutions? What constraints do we operate under and why have they come about? This section looks at the development of qualifications in the vocational and post-14 sectors. In doing so, it draws on the writings of Ecclestone (1998) and Williams and Raggatt (1998).

Summative assessment was traditionally carried out in one of two ways: by written examination or coursework in school and college, or through observation of performance in workplace situations. If we look, for example, at the early 1980s, we see a landscape of assessment of General Certificate of Education (GCE) O and A levels and Certificate of Secondary Education (CSE), some specific vocational, or technician awards, (such as those for accounting technicians, for example) and employer-based qualifications. The GCE and CSE awards were administered by a number of examination boards tied to universities and regional areas respectively. The latter, the regional boards, had begun to work with some employers to develop tests of what we now regard as key skills. Thus in the East Midlands, Rolls Royce developed numeracy tests that could be sat by school students and then used for application to the company, or elsewhere. These developments could be seen as a response to the view, prevalent then as perhaps now, that school-leavers' competence in basic skills was too low and that traditional schooling did not prepare students for the world of work (Williams and Raggatt, 1998).

The vocational, or technician, awards were awarded by the RSA, City and Guilds, and the Business and Technician Education Councils (BEC/TEC). These councils had been formed in 1974 in part response to the Haslegrave Report of five years earlier. In 1984 the two councils merged to form the BTEC. BTEC continued to develop new awards and curricula, including new versions of the National Diploma which had been around in various forms since the 1930s. It could be argued that the establishment of a single large body, complementing the RSA, City and Guilds and outside of the existing examination boards, to deal with vocational awards, led to the division between vocational and academic qualifications which successive government initiatives have tried to address. This will be discussed later (see below).

The 1985/86 Review of Vocational Qualifications in England and subsequent White Paper, *Working Together*, led to the establishment of the National Council for Vocational Qualifications (NCVQ). One of the first acts of the new Council was to establish the system of NVQs. Intended to replace the disparate range of qualifications with a unified system, the NVQs were based on competency statements echoing the philosophy of US teacher education as espoused by the MSC in their New Training Initiative (Williams and Raggatt, 1998). The review, and the concerns over employability, also led to a series of new initiatives through the second half of the 1980s and early 1990s. The MSC had been trying to tackle the unemployment of young people through work-based training and the Department of Education and Science had launched the Technical and Vocational Education Initiative (TVEI). The TVEI initiative, and later the launch of qualifications such as the Certificate of Pre-Vocational Education (CPVE) and its successor, the short-lived Diploma of Vocational Education (DVE), embodied the concept of a vocationally-related qualification that was later revamped with the launch of the GNVQs. The GNVQs and their precursors sought to bring vocational slants to education for 14–19-year-olds in parallel with the NVQ system for those who were in work. At the same time the GCE/CSE awards for 16-year-olds had been replaced by GCSEs (in 1986) and underpinned by the new National Curriculum (1987).

All of these developments radically altered the concepts of assessment for the 14–19 age group in schools and colleges. Although examinations continued, coursework and assign-ment-based activities now formed the basis of much of the assessment. This was not entirely new as CSEs had involved this approach; but the range of qualifications that now adopted some element of continuous assessment meant that all students and their teachers were affected. New approaches needed to be learned. The widespread implementation of GNVQs in schools and colleges alongside other BTEC, RSA and City and Guilds awards meant that the notion of teacher as 'assessor' became part of the professional vocabulary.

As a consequence, teachers and tutors had a more facilitative role than previously, and the students became more involved in the assessment process. The GNVQs, in particular, had notional requirements for teachers to gain the formal assessor awards (known as the D32/33) and unit specifications for these laid out very clearly the requirements for assessment and the sort of evidence that might be presented. These awards, from the Training and Development Lead Body (TDLB), had been in place for NVQ assessors, but now they were part of the landscape for school and college teachers for the 14–19 vocationally related qualifications. Assessment decisions were 'verified' both internally by other school or college staff and externally by board-appointed staff. Qualifications for verifiers (D33/34) complemented those for assessors. A key difference between verification and the well-known process of moderation was that the verifier was more concerned with the processes and approach to assessment rather than just considering the outcomes of work that had been assessed.

These clearly defined assessment requirements and assessor and verifier awards matched the NVQ model although there was, perhaps, less of an emphasis on demonstration of competencies in the GNVQ. Nevertheless, with the introduction of TDLB awards for teachers of GNVQs, the taxonomy of types of assessment evidence became part of the vocabulary of assessment for 14–19-year-olds. This taxonomy has been developed with the successive updating of the awards (the assessor's award is now known as A1, for example), but a typical list is provided by a hospital's NVQ handbook. Here evidence that may be considered for assessment is outlined in Table 6.1.

Table 6.1 List of evidence types

Naturalistic observation of (workplace) activities
Expert witness evidence
Witness testimony
Candidate reports
Reflective accounts
Assessment of prior learning/achievement
Professional discussion
Verbal/written questions
Projects/assignments/case studies
Audio/video as evidence
Product evidence
Simulation/role play – permitted in a very limited number of units and performance criteria

(adapted from Leeds Teaching Hospitals NHS Trust (undated))

The list in Table 6.1 gives an indication of the wide range of possible evidence for assessment and includes much in the way of learner involvement (for example, reflective accounts, candidate reports, professional discussion). This and the notions of transparency referred to earlier also mark a move towards the use of formative assessment and assessment for learning. If the range of types of evidence is diverse and if the students are involved in the process then it follows that the process is ongoing rather than a terminal activity, and therefore is inevitably more formative. The development of this range of types of assessment is, by definition, a portfolio approach. Portfolios are often regarded as the default product for assessment and much has been written about the use of technology for capturing and storing work in an 'e-portfolio'. It could be argued, however, that there is a danger that the technology will constrain what is captured and the portfolio will become a summative repository rather than a living record of achievement containing the diverse types of evidence listed above.

The development of general vocational qualifications (or vocationally-related qualifications as they later became) continued through the 1990s. The Capey Report (NCVQ, 1995) into assessment of GNVQs recommended greater use of external assessment. This resulted in a review and restructuring of the assessment process to incorporate more use of tests and greater similarity to the assessment processes of GCSE/GCE awards. This was partly to address what had been seen as a burdensome assessment methodology and to tackle the lack of parity of esteem.

GNVQs had been introduced to complement GCSEs and GCE A levels but increasingly they were seen as second-rate with, for example, their use as a route and preparation for university entrance not matching expectation. On the whole, universities continued to look for traditional A levels as an entry qualification, not their GNVQ level 3 equivalent. It was partly this problem which the Capey reforms were designed to address. Further changes, following the Dearing Report, came in 2000 with a unified review of the post-16 and GNVQ curricula. All general level 3 awards (GCE A levels, and the Advanced Vocational Certificate of Education (AVCE) which replaced Advanced GNVQ) were given a common six- or twelve-unit structure. Common university entrance tariffs were designed and greater similarity in assessment was introduced with unit tests across all such qualifications. In parallel with this the Diploma and Certificate awards offered by BTEC continued.

Despite these reforms, there remained a lack of parity of esteem between these vocational awards and the traditional A level, reflected in a failure to establish a wider take up of vocationally related qualifications in the 14–19 sector. As a result, following the Tomlinson Report (DfES, 2004), the GNVQ/AVCE awards were phased out to be replaced by a new suite of Diplomas aimed at 14–19-year-olds. These Diplomas are designed to encourage employer engagement, and can only be offered by consortia of providers. These would typically be a group of schools, colleges, employers and training partners working in colla-boration.

From an assessment point of view, however, the types of assessment that are used in the Diplomas are very much those listed in Table 6.1 above alongside the traditional examina-tion. An important question which this raises is whether we should allow the presence of a summative examination or test to *shape* the formative assessment opportunities we use in the classroom, or whether there are more useful models to follow among the 'menu' which Table 6.1 provides.

Conclusion

In this chapter we have looked at how assessments might be designed and implemented and we have considered an historical perspective as to how we have come to assess in the way that we do. We are now at a point at which we have very explicit assessment guidance, criteria and requirements in our qualifications specifications. We also have unified national frameworks for each of qualifications (the National Qualifications Framework (NQF)), structure of awards (as exemplified in the National Database for Accredited Qualifications (NDAQ)) and Professional Standards for teachers (see Appendix on pages 61–63). With this uniformity comes a danger that students' individual needs may not be at the forefront, although perhaps the notions of fairness discussed in this chapter should help to address this.

Moreover, teachers need to always remember that students bring with them a wealth of prior experience and knowledge and that their lives beyond school or college also provide ranges of contexts in which learning may be demonstrated. Teaching, learning and assess-ment need to be open to these ranges of contexts so that assessment of students' capability is as authentic as it can be, as meaningful to students and others as it can be and robust enough to deflect any criticisms of its veracity.

References

Biggs, P (1999) *Teaching for quality learning at university.* Buckingham: Open University Press.

Black, P, Harrison, C, Lee, C, Marshall, B and Wiliam, D (2003). *Assessment for learning: putting it into practice.* Buckingham: Open University Press.

Black, P and Wiliam, D (1998) *Inside the black box: raising standards through classroom assessment.* London: NFER Nelson.

Black, P and Wiliam, D (2006) The reliability of assessments, in Gardner, J (ed). *Assessment and learning.* London: Sage, pp119–32.

DfES (2004) *14–19 curriculum and qualifications reform: final report of the working group on 14–19 reform.* London: Department for Education and Skills.

Ecclestone, K (2004) *Learning autonomy in post-16 education.* London: Routledge.

Gardner, J (ed) (2006) *Assessment and learning.* London: Sage.

Goodwin, A (ed) (1997) *Assessment for equity and inclusion: embracing all our children.* London: Routledge.

Harlen, W (2007) *Assessment of learning.* London: Sage.

James, M and Pedder, D (2006). Professional learning as a condition for assessment for learning, in Gardner, J (ed) *Assessment and learning.* London: Sage, pp27–44.

Leeds Teaching Hospitals NHS Trust (undated) NVQ handbook. Available: **www.leedsth.nhs.uk/ sites/nvq/NVQHandbook.php** (accessed November 2009).

LLUK (2007) *Professional standards for teachers in the Lifelong Learning sector.* London: Lifelong Learning UK.

LSIS (2005) *Assessment for learning.* Coventry: Learning and Skills Information Service (Vocational Learning Support Programme).

Mulder, R and Sloane, P (eds) (2004) *New approaches to vocational education in Europe.* Oxford: Symposium Books.

NCVQ (1995) *GNVQ assessment review (The Capey Report).* London: National Council for Vocational Qualifications.

OECD (2006) *Improving schooling: personalising education.* Paris: Organisation for Economic Co-operation and Development.

Stobart, G (2006) The validity of formative assessment, in Gardner, J (ed). *Assessment and learning.* London: Sage, pp133–46.

Stobart, G and Gipps, C (1997) *Assessment: a teacher's guide to the issues* (3rd edn.) London: Hodder and Stoughton.

Tombari, M and Borich, G (1999) *Authentic assessment in the classroom: applications and practice.* Columbus, OH: Merrill.

University of Roehampton (undated) *Good practice in assessment.* Available at **www.roehampton. ac.uk/guidetogoodpracticeinassessment/index.html** (accessed November 2009).

Williams, S and Raggatt, P (1998) Contextualising public policy in vocational education and training: the origins of competence-based vocational qualifications policy in the UK. *Journal of Education and Work,* 11(3): 275–92.

Appendix: The Professional Standards relating to Assessment and Reflection (a summary from all relevant areas of the standards)

Teachers in the LLS are committed to designing and using assessment as a tool for learning and progression (ES1).

They value learners, their progress and development, their learning goals and aspirations (AS1). They know and understand:

- theories and principles of assessment and the application of different forms of assessment including;
    - initial;
    - formative;
    - summative (EK 1.1)
- ways to devise, select, use and appraise assessment tools, including, where appropriate, those which exploit new and emerging technologies (EK 1.2);
- the principles of assessment design in relation to own specialist area (EK 2.3);
- ways to ensure access to assessment within a learning programme (EK3.2);
- the relevance of learning approaches, preferences and skills to learner progress (BK 2.3);
- a range of listening and questioning techniques to support learning (BK 3.2).

They:

- use appropriate forms of assessment and evaluate their effectiveness in producing information useful to the teacher and the learner (EP 1.1);
- devise, select, use and appraise assessment tools, including where appropriate, those which exploit new and emerging technologies (EP 1.2);
- design appropriate assessment activities for own specialist area (EP 2.3);
- use assessment information to promote learning through questioning and constructive feedback, and involve learners in feedback activities (EP 4.1);
- use listening and questioning techniques appropriately and effectively in a range of learning contexts (BP 3.2);
- plan teaching sessions which meet the aims and needs of individual learners and groups, using a variety of resources, including new and emerging technologies (DP 1.2);
- plan for opportunities for learner feedback to inform planning and practice (DP 2.1).

Teachers in the LLS are committed to assessing the work of learners in a fair and equitable manner (ES2).

They know and understand:

- issues of equality and diversity in assessment (EK 2.1);
- concepts of validity, reliability and sufficiency in assessment (EK 2.2).

They:

- apply appropriate methods of assessment fairly and effectively (EP 2.1);
- apply appropriate assessment methods to produce valid, reliable and sufficient evidence (EP 2.2);
- ensure that access to assessment is appropriate to learner need (EP 3.2);

Teachers in the LLS are committed to learner involvement and shared responsibility in the assessment process (ES3).

They are committed:

- to applying and developing own professional skills to enable learners to achieve their goals (BS2);
- to communicating effectively and appropriately with learners to enhance learning (BS3);
- to learner participation in the planning of learning (DS2).

They know and understand:

- ways to develop, establish and promote peer- and self-assessment (EK 1.3);
- ways to establish learner involvement in and personal responsibility for assessment of their learning (EK3.1);
- the role of feedback and questioning in assessment for learning (EK 4.1);
- what motivates learners to learn and the importance of learners' experience and aspirations (AK 1.1);
- ways to engage, motivate and encourage active participation of learners and learner independence (BK 2.2);
- ways of using learners' own experiences as a foundation for learning (BK 2.5);
- the importance of including learners in the planning process (DK 2.1);
- ways to negotiate appropriate individual goals with learners (DK 2.2).

They:

- develop, establish and promote peer- and self-assessment as a tool for learning and progression (EP1.3);
- ensure that learners understand, are involved and share in responsibility for assessment of their learning (EP 3.1);
- create a motivating environment which encourages learners to reflect on, evaluate and make decisions about their learning (BP 1.3);
- use a range of effective and appropriate teaching and learning techniques to engage and motivate learners

and encourage independence (BP 2.2);
- encourage learners to use their own life experiences as a foundation for their development (BP 2.5);
- negotiate and record appropriate learning goals and strategies with learners (DP 2.2).

Teachers in the LLS are committed to using feedback as a tool for learning and progression (ES4).
They:
- value reflection and evaluation of their own practice (AS4);
- know and understand the role of feedback in effective evaluation and improvement of own assessment skills (EK 4.2).

They:
- use feedback to evaluate and improve own skills in assessment (EP4.2).
- encourage the development and progression of all learners through recognising, valuing and responding to individual motivation, experience and aspirations (AP 1.1).

Teachers in the LLS are committed to working within the systems and quality requirements of the organisation in relation to assessment and monitoring of learner progress (ES5).
They know and understand:
- how to work as part of a team to establish equitable assessment processes (EK2.4);
- the necessary/appropriate assessment information to communicate to others who have a legitimate interest in learner achievement (EK5.3);
- the role of assessment and associated organisational procedures in relation to the quality cycle (EK5.1);
- the assessment requirements of individual learning programmes and procedures for conducting and recording internal and/or external assessments (EK5.2).

They:
- collaborate with others, as appropriate, to promote equity and consistency in assessment processes (EP 2.4);
- contribute to the organisation's quality cycle by producing accurate and standardised assessment information, and keeping appropriate records of assessment decisions and learners' progress (EP 5.1);
- conduct and record assessments which adhere to the particular requirements of individual learning programmes and, where appropriate, external bodies (EP 5.2);
- communicate relevant assessment information to those with a legitimate interest in learner achievement, as necessary/appropriate (EP 5.3).

Professional skills for reading and writing

This section aims to support and extend your understanding of the text, and to highlight some of the conventions of formal academic writing. It focuses on the conventions governing the use of appendices in formal writing.

1 The purpose and positioning of appendices
The purpose of an appendix is to provide the reader with more detailed information or context which will add to their understanding of the text but which would disrupt the flow or take up too much space if incorporated into the text itself. Consider, for example, why the

writer has placed his digest of assessment-related standards in an appendix, but has placed the Table 6.1 in the body of the text.

If you are using an appendix or several appendices to support your text you should place them at the end of your paper or assignment, *after* the references, as this writer demonstrates here.

2 Using the appendices effectively

An appendix is only useful and necessary if you are going to make reference to it in your text. The addition of appendices to a piece of writing which contains no reference to them at all is not acceptable practice. If you look through this paper again you will see that in several places the writer directs the reader to the appendix in order to find more detail or a fuller version of something he has mentioned in the text. In this paper it is, in each case, a reference to the Professional Standards for LLS teachers on assessment. Therefore only that one appendix is necessary.

3 Identifying appendices

If, however, you need to include more than one appendix it is essential that you identify each one clearly, both as a heading to each appendix itself and on each occasion that you refer to it in your text, for example: (see Appendix 1) or (see Appendix 2) and so on.

Discussion

These discussion tasks will help you to explore the relevance of this paper to your own professional practice.

DISCUSSION TASK

Assessment design

Consider a unit or module of work which you teach in the light of the issues raised in this chapter. Any such unit will have a defined set of assessment requirements. You should start by listing these and then consider whether they are sufficient to meet the needs of students and other stakeholders.

How well does the assessment align with the learning objectives? Is what is being assessed appropriate, necessary and sufficient to allow coverage of the objectives to be measured? Does the product and method of assessment allow students to demonstrate the knowledge, understanding, skills and attributes that they have acquired through studying the unit?

For other stakeholders there are questions of ease of use and of authenticity. To what extent do the outcomes of the assessments translate into something that is understood by those who might need to interpret them? If you were a teacher taking the group after they had been assessed on your unit, would the results be helpful in informing you what the students knew, understood and could do? If you were an employer, what would you expect the students to be able to do if they had achieved a certain result in the unit?

Having done this check of alignment, usefulness and authenticity you should then go on to consider issues of reliability, validity and fairness. To what extent can you demonstrate that these are addressed by the assessment methods in your unit? What evidence do you have for such assertions?

So far the discussion of design here has focused on the 'requirements'. Perhaps you have only considered summative assessment as this is what is most often defined. What then, are the opportunities and activities for formative assessment in the unit?

DISCUSSION TASK

Learner involvement

Having discussed the ways in which your assessments are designed and the opportunities they provide for formative and summative assessment you should now consider the learners' involvement in the process. To what extent do they engage in self-assessment, peer-assessment and reflection? Do you build in opportunities for negotiation and target setting following formative assessments? Is there any similar activity after the unit is complete to allow learners to reflect on the whole unit before embarking on the next with some synoptic lessons and targets?

DISCUSSION TASK

The reflective practitioner and the LLUK Professional Standards

Having considered the assessment from the perspective of the learner and other stakeholders you should now consider how you use the opportunities to inform your own practice. To what extent do you gather feedback from assessment – whether formative or summative – to help with your own development and the development of the unit or module? Similarly, do you make use of any formal and informal evaluations from students and do you have any systems for recording your own reflections?

The Professional Standards refer to assessment and reflection in a number of domains as discussed in the introduction to this chapter. The Appendix summarises all of these references. You may find it useful to use this as a checklist to see how your use of assessment and reflection processes in the unit you are considering helps you to meet the Professional Standards. Are there things which you do that run counter to them or are there ways in which you would amend or improve them?

FURTHER READING FURTHER READING **FURTHER READING** FURTHER READING

An overview of assessment issues in post-14 education is provided by the booklet from LSIS (2005). Although less in-depth than the sources listed in the References, it provides a useful starting point.

The Assessment Reform Group has been researching the ways in which assessment impacts on learning and teaching for over 20 years. It has produced a wealth of publications including the writing of Black and Wiliam (1998) referenced earlier. While these authors concentrate on Assessment for Learning, the counterpart Assessment of Learning is explored by Harlen (2007).

An international perspective, set in the context of personalising education, is provided by OECD (2006) and Mulder and Sloane (2004).

Finally, although written for HE, the guide from the University of Roehampton (undated) contains a wealth of practical information for teachers when considering approaches to assessment.

7
Professionalism and reflective practice

The aims of the chapter are to provide:

- an example of an academic writing style;
- a review of some of the theory and uses of reflective practice in lifelong learning;
- a demonstration of the links between reflective practice and action research;
- a way of increasing understanding about the ways in which reflective and critically reflexive practices enhance professionalism.

What to look for

- Observe how the research and literature is used to present the overall discussion about reflective practice and professionalism.
- Consider how the arguments are presented and note where the author has a particular bias towards one perspective or another. What elements in the writing create this impression?
- Take time as you read to reflect on your own perspective about the various arguments and discussions. You may like to consider the following questions:
  - What motivates *you* to reflect on your practice?
  - How often is it driven by a work problem or challenge?
  - Where are you best able to reflect?
  - What do you hope/expect to get out of the reflective process?

Key words: reflective practice, critical reflexive practice, reflection, action research, professionalism

Author details

Kate Kennett has been involved in the research and development of reflective practice in public sector settings for many years. Currently, she works as a consultant for reflect4change, a small business specialising in supporting organisations to establish reflective practice in their professional learning and development portfolio. Her current research interest is in the impact of reflective practice groups as a means for providing support to Learning Mentors.

Professionalism and reflective practice

Kate Kennett

Abstract

This paper provides an introduction to reflective practice in the LLS and presents a rationale for how it has become an important feature of CPD with the purpose of enhancing professionalism. It explores reflective practice theory and considers some of the challenges of transferring the theory into professional practice. The psychological dimensions associated with being an effective reflective practitioner are considered in order to understand some of the potential barriers to engagement. Several approaches to support participation in reflective and reflexive practices are suggested, including an introduction to action research methodology.

Introduction

Professionals who work in FE come from a variety of backgrounds, and frequently enter teaching through non-traditional routes. Whatever their individual circumstance, common to them all is that they have chosen to work in the sector primarily because they possess expertise, skills and knowledge in specialist vocational and/or academic disciplines (Davies, 2006). Already experts in their specialist field, many are now in the process of developing 'dual-professionalism' as they engage in the process of communicating what they know to other learners in the same field through their teaching practice.

Reflective practice is a key element of all teacher training programmes including the field of LLS. However, from it being recognised as good practice, it is now a requirement to reflect for CPD. The Institute for Learning states that: *Reflective Practice – taking personal responsibility to improve professional practice through thinking about practice, discussion with colleagues and learners and taking appropriate action to improve – is required of all teachers* (Lifelong Learning UK, 2009, p12).

A teacher working full time is expected to demonstrate at least 30 hours of CPD every year. More than simply attending training events, or participating in courses (even Masters Degree level), reflection on the experience, evaluation of the findings and keeping a record of these reflections is an additional requirement. But reflection of any sort is not straightforward and does not occur as an inevitable by-product of being a professional in the workplace. It requires the learning of key skills to engage effectively in ways that lead to positive outcomes (Schön, 1991; Argyris, 1999; Gray, 2007; Marcos et al, 2009). It requires determined effort and ongoing commitment (as well as the motivation) to prioritise what must feel like an additional work activity in an already demanding schedule.

Reflective practice is a term much bandied about and, in many ways, little understood. There is no single, universally agreed definition that neatly provides a generic explanation of reflective practice. However, there are many distinguished thinkers and writers in the field who have made significant contributions to the current debate. As a learning process, reflecting on practice is unlike traditional education methods, in which the outcomes of learning are largely predictable and expected. Turning experience into learning requires not just commitment, but often a supportive structure, framework or model in which to unravel the experience and make sense of it. This may include other people with whom to interact and share the discoveries.

Much of the literature enthusiastically encourages reflection on experiences in teaching, occasionally providing a framework for the practice. It largely assumes that by so doing, it will enhance the professionalism of the practitioner by automatically transferring the new knowledge, skills and expertise into front line teaching practice. Considerably less is written about the barriers to engaging in reflective practice, or even providing convincing evidence about the quality and outcomes of the activity. In the same way that we understand and accept that students have a range of learning styles and may experience a whole gamut of problems and individual difficulties, so too do teachers. It is one thing to reflect on experiences that occur and attempt to place them in a frame of understanding; it is another for teachers to produce transformative learning that impacts on and improves practice.

This chapter provides an introduction to reflective practice in the education sector and discusses how it has become an important feature in continuing professional learning and development. It takes account of relevant psychological factors and barriers that impact on the potential for reflection on practice to be transferred effectively into the professional work setting. The paradigmatic shift from reflective to critical reflexive practice is considered in relation to a reflective practice taxonomy.

The origins of reflective practice

Reflective practice is as old as philosophical thought, with Socrates (ca 469 BC–399 BC) often being credited as one of the first proponents. Socrates's lifework consisted of the examination of his own and other people's lives. He pursued this task single-mindedly, asking people around him questions about what mattered most to them. His favoured subjects included issues of courage, love, objects of worship, moral values, and the state of people's souls generally. He later declared at his trial for impiety (disrespecting the gods and corrupting the youth) that: *the unexamined life is not worth living for a human being,* (Plato, undated). His process of asking questions, more questions and ever more questions is, in many ways, still a fail-safe approach to engaging in reflective practice.

Rather more recently, Dewey (1910; 1991), one of the original heavyweights of reflective thought in the field of education, coined a definition that is widely quoted. He considered that: *active, persistent and careful consideration of any belief or supposed form of knowledge in the light of the grounds that support it and the further conclusion to which it tends, constitutes reflective thought* (p6). This was certainly a forerunner to what followed in the field and many writers still cite him as a critical contributor to reflective theory and practice. In the 1980s, several distinguished writers explored the subject of reflective thought and practice. Schön (1991), in *The Reflective Practitioner*, proposed that the technical aspects of professional training only allow for core knowledge and skills to be learned and that this type of knowledge was inadequate to prepare professionals to deal with the type of complex challenges that they would face in their normal professional practice. By splitting off theory from practice, he thought that this narrow approach to training ill-prepared professionals to recognise or value other qualities, such as wisdom and common sense.

The settings in which teachers operate are – more than most professions – unpredictable and require a certain fleetness of foot. Schön (1991) referred to this type of arena as the *swampy lowland where situations are confusing 'messes' incapable of technical solution* (p42). This *swampy lowland* is a place in which, to do more than merely survive, professionals will need to use their intuition, creativity and the wisdom born of human experience, in tandem with the arsenal of their technical knowledge and skills. By engaging in a reflective practice process the practitioner has an opportunity to step back and occupy a different perspective from which to make sense of the contents of the swamp. Schön's (1983) hypothesis was that if professionals regularly engaged in reflective thought and actions, the increased knowledge would *develop and improve their practice, making it more responsive to their clients' needs* even if this means letting go of some of the kudos gained from occupying the role of authoritative expert (Redmond, 2006, p39).

What are reflective practices?

Boud et al (1985) edited an excellent collection of essays in their book *Reflection: Turning Experience into Learning.* This brought together a number of writers who, for the first time, presented their ideas about reflection in learning and considered how this can be facilitated. They offer a much quoted definition of reflection: *it is an active process of exploration and discovery which often leads to very unexpected outcomes* (p7) ... *not idle meanderings or day-dreaming, but purposive activity directed towards a goal* (p11). This makes it *an important human activity in which people recapture their experience, think about it, mull it over and evaluate it* (p18).

Perhaps stating the obvious, they also note the following.

- *Only learners themselves can learn and only they can reflect on their own experiences* (p11). In other words, their point is, that no one else has access to anyone else's thoughts, feelings and experiences upon which to reflect and analyse. While this makes it an individual pursuit in which each person must determine their own approach and particular process of engagement, it is not necessarily a solitary process.
- It is purposeful and deliberate – rather than an accidental by-product of daydreaming, or thought wandering; it is both goal focused and critical. An evaluation process is crucial to complete the cycle of experiential reflective learning.
- It is a highly complex activity involving a whole range of thoughts and emotions. This aspect recognises that negative feelings can be a serious barrier to learning and that nurturing a positive sense of self is a vital step towards transformative learning.

Mezirow (1991) wrote a groundbreaking book, *Transformative Dimensions of Adult Learning,* in which he considered reflection to be the process by which we *critically assess the content, process or premise of our efforts to interpret and give meaning to an experience* (p104). He proposed that reflection is fundamental to experience-based learning, in which prior knowledge, skills and experiences become a resource for professional development; *the goal of reflective learning is a* transformation of perspective *– a significant shift in perspective that allows professionals not only to critically review their practice, but which also helps them to work in a more responsive, creative, and ultimately more effective manner* (p1). This, in many ways, defined what has come to be known as the raison d'être for critical reflective practice, paving the way towards a more complex level of reflection: critical reflexivity.

Raelin (2001) described reflection as the practice of *periodically stepping back to ponder the meaning to self and to others in one's immediate environment about what has recently transpired* (p11) and of encouraging critical and innovative thinking that supports competent and meaningful professional practice. This descriptor makes both the process and the purpose for reflection on practice clear and simple. It also leaves open how the process is undertaken, which presents a challenge for the novice reflector.

Why engage in reflective practices?

Generally speaking, the purpose for participating in some form of reflection on practice is far more than compliance with QTLS standards and CPD requirements. It is associated with multiple benefits that are provided by committing to a regular practice of reflection on professional experience. In professional learning environments, reflection is a key element to reach *deeper meaning of what is being taught and learned beyond the actual purposed or function* (Hackett, 2001 p103). Schön's hypothesis was that when professionals reflect on their practice, the subsequent insights and learning will feed back into and improve their practice. *Reflective teaching and learning is not confined to the acquisition of new skills, rather it creates an environment where professionals are helped to analyse and re-apprise their practice* (Redmond, 2006 p1).

Ghaye (2008) believes that there is a real risk of becoming *fashion victims* if attention is focused on the *concept* of reflective practice, rather than having a considered rationale for using it or understanding its potential value. He argues that if it follows a robust methodology – that is, if it is done in a systematic and rigorous way – it can and does lead to improvements in three key areas for the individual's:

1. feelings about work and working life;
2. thoughts about work and working life; and
3. actions in particular workplaces.

His evidence base is derived from a number of sources including personal experience, others' published experiences, a growing volume of research literature in the field and a rising number of national and international conferences on this area of practice.

These suggest that the benefits of reflection on practice include:

- the ability to stand back and observe situations and retrospectively, ask critical questions that lead to the development of new knowledge and skills;
- increased awareness and understanding about experience;
- new perspectives on situations experienced in the 'swampy lowlands' of professional practice;
- a sense of empowerment and increased capacity to make decisions and manage change;
- development of staff who find creative, practical and effective solutions to external demands and challenges;
- the ability to design and implement improvement strategies;
- the development of emotionally intelligent, effective and professional communicators;
- improved confidence and increased professionalism in the role of being a teacher in the classroom.

How does reflection on practice enhance professionalism?

The concept of professionalism is discussed by Roffey-Barentsen and Malthouse (2009) in their useful book *Reflective Practice in the Lifelong Learning Sector* where they suggest that professionalism is a consequence of several combined factors including *the setting of high standards, by maintaining appropriate specialist knowledge, and by shared values* (p15). Marcos et al (2009) propose that central to most ideas presented in research literature is that *through reflection the teacher better understands and extends his/her professional activity, and that reflecting on teaching problems will lead to new insights for practice*, with the overall benefit of this scrutinising process being an enrichment, systematising and reconstruction of professional knowledge (p191).

Davies (2006) also proposes a number of criteria to define professionalism including:

- making professional development an ongoing process that adds value throughout a teaching practitioner's career;

- assessing the value of a training and development activity in terms of its impact on teaching – not in the time taken to complete the activity;
- putting the teaching practitioner at the centre of the CPD process, responsible for reflecting on practice and identifying their own personal development needs;
- having professional development plans that clearly articulate the needs of the teaching practitioner, setting measurable objectives that reflect the teaching context and synthesise with the needs of the employer;
- seeking a balance between formal and informal CPD activities, relative to the needs of the teaching practitioner at that point in their career;
- seeing professional development as an integral element of all work activity, rather than a burdensome add-on.

To this, I would add that there are several intrinsic factors – personal motivators, attributes and attitudes associated with being a professional in the workplace. These include making an explicit commitment to having an attitude of openness to new possibilities and perspectives about professional knowledge and skills and how these may be most effectively communicated. They also involve developing a conscious awareness that, while almost inevitably mistakes will be made, so too successes will occur. It is about what the individual does in the wake of making a mistake, or achieving success and whether they seek to understand and learn from the experience, that helps to define them as a professional.

Levels of reflection on practice

Boud et al (1985) observed that *the capacity to reflect is developed to different stages in different people* (p19). Many models for understanding reflectivity (Mezirow 1981; Boyd and Fales, 1983; Goodmans, 1984) and frameworks for engaging in forms of structured reflection (for example, Kennett, 2006) have been developed. These all indicate that individuals engage at different levels when participating in reflective practice activities. In her discussion about critical reflexivity, Cunliffe (2004) observes that the reflective practitioner makes a *gradual move* from a process that is relatively simple, to one that is considerably more complex. This sense of progression through different *levels* of reflectivity has been further explored through the construction of a reflective taxonomy (Kennett, 2006). This identifies six levels that are marked by an increasingly more complex process of reflective activity (see Figure 7.1 on page 72). One important function of the taxonomy is that it fundamentally challenges the assumption that the starting place for an individual engaging in a form of reflective practice is the same for everyone. From Kennett's MSc research findings, several interesting factors became apparent about the level at which individuals engaged in reflective thinking. These appeared to be influenced by many environmental, social and psychological factors, not least the culture of the work setting. Similarly, Platzer et al (2000) noted that the degree to which openness to ideas, the tolerance of challenges to authority and encouragement to subject personal actions to scrutiny were supported by the employer, inevitably influenced the degree of reflective behaviour among employees.

Let us look now in some detail at the taxonomy showing different levels of reflectivity illustrated in Figure 7.1 below.

Reactive/non-reflective behaviour and thinking

The base of the taxonomy is marked by the non-reflective and reactive behaviours described by the educational settings of the participants in the research study. These include the repetition of habitual responses to similar situations rather than examining each situation for its different and defining characteristics; exhibiting an extreme urgency to act precipitously and with little critical thinking; inadequate time allocated to think about actions or consider other possibilities and options in situations; or an excessive need to assert power and control over staff. At this level, the organisation, as much as the individual staff employed within it, is not reflecting or demonstrating learning behaviours.

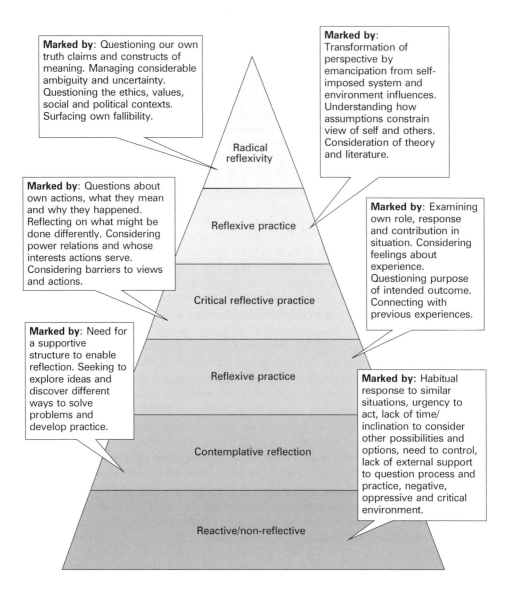

Figure 7.1 Reflective taxonomy

(Kennett, 2006)

Contemplative reflection

At this level, there is a dawning awareness of the benefits and value that reflective behaviour may contribute. Some initial exploration and testing out of different reflective possibilities may occur. There may be an intellectual recognition of the requirement for a supportive infrastructure to enable or facilitate reflection on practice, systems and processes and a need to change the culture of the organisation to support a different way of thinking and learning.

Reflective practice

This was the entry level for many of the participants in the research project. In facilitated reflective practice groups, they examined their own role, response and contribution to different situations using a simple problem-solving framework (Kennett, 2006). They considered what they thought and how they felt about work-based experiences. With the support of other group members, they asked and were asked questions about the context and circumstances of the experience and considered their choices for taking action. At this level, they operated with single-loop learning (Argyris, 1991) to logically problem solve, rather than analyse causal factors linked to the issue or test underpinning assumptions.

Critical reflective practice

This level operates with a more analytic approach to reflection in which individuals ask questions about their own actions, what they mean and why they happened. This may be undertaken in a wide range of different ways including storytelling, use of reflective metaphors, coaching and mentoring (Cunliffe, 2004; Gray, 2006). They also question wider behaviour and external impacts, evaluate what might be done differently and consciously draw learning from the analysis. This level uses double-loop learning (Argyris, 1991) in which they think critically about their espoused theories in contrast to their theory-in-action.

Reflexive practice

Engagement in reflexive practice is marked by the complex and extensive consideration of the inter-relationship between self, others and the operating context. It intends to expand and develop a deep understanding about how assumptions constrain and limit the view of self and others. The frame of reference incorporates a depth examination of underlying assumptions, priorities and influences in the wider field. The intended outcome is less 'solving of a problem' than transformation of perspective by emancipation from self-imposed systems and environmental influences. Frequent reference is made to associated theory and literature.

Radical reflexivity

This level is marked by an *awareness of self-awareness* (Rennie, 2006), questioning of own and others' truth claims, and seeking to analyse the constructs of meaning in all matters. It involves the management of considerable ambiguity and uncertainty, questioning the ethics, values, and social and political contexts of every situation. At a psychological level, it aims to surface our own fallibility by an existential exploration of the concepts of moral evaluation and freedom of will. All relationships are defined according to their power differential and the impact of preconscious determinants. The activity involved in radical reflexive practice includes the widest range of verbal, visual/artistic and written forms of expression.

Barriers and challenges to reflecting on practice

There are multiple complex features that occur in all levels of reflective activity including feelings and cognitions. Boud et al (1985) suggest that it is the negative feelings about oneself that *can form major barriers to learning* (p11) and effectively distort, disrupt and undermine the potential to reflect on learning. Unfortunately, when people make mistakes, they are often overwhelmed with preoccupying emotions that are confusing, if not actually negative, in quality. In such situations, a common defence mechanism is to turn away from, rather than towards, the experience. Yet arguably, some of our most valuable learning is drawn from reflection on our mistakes. If reflective practice is to result in enhanced professionalism, it is important to resist the temptation to resort to defensive manoeuvres such as burying our heads in the sand. It is one thing to try to resist the temptation to do any number of things that we find compelling; it is another to raise our level of self-awareness to recognise the underlying motives for such behaviours. In order to reflect effectively on practice, it is important to understand some of the psychological factors that motivate our own and others' learning.

This awareness of our mental models is fundamental to understanding how we plan, implement and review the actions that we take in most situations (Argyris, 1999). These often unacknowledged models or ideas influence our actions far more than the theories that we espouse (tell others we believe); and we need to recognise them if we want to identify the defensive routines that prevent us from learning from our experiences. Ultimately, they can motivate us to, or inhibit us from, making decisions and taking action to make changes in many aspects of our lives, including teaching practice. Indeed, Argyris (1999) suggests that an individual's sense of competence, self-confidence and self-esteem are inextricably connected with the way that they think and interpret information at a very deep level. This makes it immensely difficult for the individual to see for themselves how entrenched their behaviour may have become, how their tacit beliefs and values dictate their actions and as a consequence, limit their learning and practice.

One function of our participation in reflective practice is that we begin to realise the distinction between what we *say* we believe (our espoused theory) and what we *do* (our theories-in-use). Argyris (1999) suggests that effective learning is the consequence of developing congruence between the two positions – bringing the two together. A challenge for the reflective process is to increase our awareness of this discrepancy between what we say and what we do, to reveal our underlying theory-in-use. This can be achieved by asking critical questions about the extent to which our actual behaviour aligns with our espoused theory and to what degree our inner feelings, beliefs and values emerge through our actions and practice. However, while reflective activity can offer unrivalled potential for improvement in the professional practice of teaching, there is evidence to suggest that the threat to our sense of identity in so doing, can lead us to keep our theory-in-use stubbornly unchanged (Argyris and Schön, 1974).

The Teacher Reflection on Action study

The 'Teacher Reflection on Action' study (Marcos et al, 2009) focused on the relationship between the claims about key theoretical elements of reflection on practice compared to the feedback from teachers about the actual value and contribution to practice. The findings seriously question the degree to which the insights from reflective practice actually make their way into professional practice – or put another way, whether the talk does eventually lead to the walk. In fact, the findings from the research study indicated that a mere 0–10 per cent of teachers actually carried out the complete cycle of reflecting on practice. In another study, none of the sample group of teachers demonstrated the ability to establish clear goals and evaluate results for practice (Butler, et al, 2004). McLellan (2004) found that 2 per cent of the sample of 40 teachers were aware of the action research cycle of steps, which can be summarised as: identifying a problem, goal-setting, solving the problem and evaluating. Tillema (2006) indicated that 10 per cent of the teachers made some reference to following a cyclical reflective process that included problem solving and goal setting. In another study, the teachers were specifically trained in an action research process. The findings showed that in this example, 70 per cent reflected by setting goals and evaluating the results. Their training particularly focused on *how* to reflect, rather than just an explanation about *what* varieties of reflective practice models exist. Interestingly, most of the studies focused on the teacher's thoughts and beliefs, as opposed to what they physically do in practice.

These studies have huge implications for any setting in which active engagement in reflective practice is required in order to maintain professional standards and for CPD. They suggest that it is one thing to legislate that individuals should engage in a regulated number of reflective practice hours, but quite another to gauge the quality of this engagement and the potential transferability of new learning into professional practice.

Overcoming the barriers to reflective learning

A number of important issues are raised by the findings of the Marcos et al (2009) study, not least the significance of the most effective ways to reflect on practice. This is vital if the much-hoped-for new learning is to have a chance of finding its way into professional practice. There are many possibilities for engaging in the process of reflection, but whether they are effective at bringing about transferable improvement into practice is subject to almost as many variables. One of these is the need to identify the *point* at which the individual engages in reflection and the most appropriate *type* of activity and support that would benefit them and enable them to reflect on their practice effectively. Marcos et al (2009) viewed the processes of action research and reflection on action as fundamentally linked. For them, reflection is modelled as a problem-solving process consisting of two connected components: action and thought. These join knowledge and action within a cycle, or series of stages that include:

- a defined problem or issue;
- an action plan;
- action taken by the teacher (the doing of the research);
- observing and studying the effects of the action;
- a review of the potential solutions (evaluation).

Action research methodology can provide a useful structure in which to undertake most forms of reflective practices. Research indicates that formal learning of the staged action research process can lead to increased likelihood of new learning finding its way into professional practice. For Ghaye, et al (2008) *An action research process often starts with an individual practitioner reflecting on an aspect of their work and looking for areas where changes might be made* (p363). Action research fundamentally engages with the problem being examined and asks what the researcher can do about it – an approach that challenges research paradigms which claim the researcher should be an impartial scientist in the process of inquiry. Through action research, taken-for-granted assumptions, values and beliefs may be interrogated and repositioned in the light of new evidence. Figure 7.2 provides an example of a very simple action research framework that can be used to carry out individual research cycles.

PLAN	Date:
What is the focus for your reflection and why?	
What possible outcomes do you want?	
What is your first step (must take no more than 10 days)?	

DO
What did you do? Where? When? With whom?

REFLECT
What happened/improved as a consequence of what you did?
Were there any unexpected outcomes?

ACT
What are you going to do next? What is your next step?

Figure 7.2 Reflective practice action cycle

The practicalities of being a reflective practitioner

There is a variety of ways to engage in reflective practice that take account of individual learning preferences. The following examples differ in the degree of social interaction involved. For example, journal writing can be undertaken independently, while working with a mentor or in a group increases the degree of social interaction involved. What they both have in common is that they contribute to making sense of experience and help to create order in complex and challenging situations. In one way or another, all those listed below do this through enabling the telling of the story of what is happening and encouraging us to share the meanings that are to be found in them (Gray, 2006).

Journal writing

Writing or keeping a form of journal can provide a powerful method to enable learners to develop their reflective and critically reflexive skills. These can incorporate a gradual move from a simple reflective process to one that is much more reflexive. Cunliffe (2004) suggests that *journals can be used to improve writing skills, improve analytic and creative thinking and build self-awareness* (p418). She suggests that starting the process requires the surfacing of assumptions and identification of behaviour patterns, values and defensive routines. It can then move to a critically reflexive position to question the origins and thinking systems in which they are situated, the impacts and influences in our professional practice. This is a far from comfortable activity and it can be helpful to utilise a framework to support the process (ibid).

However, it could present considerable challenges for those who may prefer a more interactive means of engaging in reflection.

Mentoring

At any level, mentoring can provide a highly responsive, flexible and supportive structure through which to engage both in reflective and reflexive practice. There are multiple benefits to this process. An experienced mentor is able to provide a springboard into a formal or informal reflective process and offer encouragement and feedback to reflective journal efforts. They can provide invaluable challenges to blind spots, help to surface tacit assumptions, overcome defensive routines and provide overall structure to the process (see Gravells, 2010; Garvey et al, 2009; Clutterbuck, 2004; Daloz, 1999).

Reflective practice groups

Engaging in a reflective practice group offers similar benefits to mentoring, while also providing an opportunity for collaborative learning, support and challenge with and from other professionals in the same field. The added value of having a facilitator can support participants in reviewing and challenging their prevailing knowledge base, belief system and underlying assumptions (Raelin, 2008). While this approach offers a greater diversity of skills, knowledge and experience into the reflective milieu, it can also increase the chances of conflict arising as a result of differences of viewpoints and challenging group dynamics. Skilful facilitation and the establishment of ground rules together with the commitment of the participants help to ensure that it provides a powerful learning experience.

Conclusion

Just as people start from different places as reflective practitioners, so too reflective practice can be experienced in varying degrees of complexity. As we have seen in Figure 7.1 on page 72, it can be useful to understand these as levels in a framework that shows a progressively more complex, multi-dimensional process from non-reflection through to radically reflexive practice. Each level is marked by different thinking processes, intensity of questioning and powerful challenges to individual core assumptions. As a learning process, reflecting on practice is unlike traditional education methods, in which the outcomes of learning are largely predictable and expected. There is a wide range of ways in which to reflect on practice, each offering its own particular benefits. While it is often thought of as a writing-based activity that occurs largely in private, it can, in fact, be very social and interactive, often proving most effective when it involves sharing and receiving feedback from others such as a mentor or as a participant in a reflective practice group.

Reflective practice is an important feature of CPD which adds value throughout a teaching practitioner's career. There is a substantial body of literature about reflective practice that suggests the contribution it can make to professionalism. However, while it has the potential to enhance our professional practice, there are significant factors that may create barriers to engaging in it. We should avoid the assumption that just because reflective practice is a requirement for professional development, it automatically and effortlessly becomes transferred into and embedded into professional practice. Turning experience into learning is far from inevitable and requires not just commitment, but often a supportive structure, framework or model in which to unravel experience, make sense of it and draw on it to shape our future practice.

References

Argyris, C (1991) Teaching smart people how to learn. *Harvard Business Review* 1991 May–June; 98–105.

Argyris, C (1999) *On organisational learning*. Oxford: Blackwell Publishing.

Argyris, C and Schön, D (1974) *Theory in practice: increasing professional effectiveness*. San Francisco: Jossey-Bass.

Boud, D, Keogh, R and Walker, D (eds) (1985) *Reflection: turning experience into learning*. London: RoutledgeFalmer.

Boyd, E and Fales, A (1983) Reflective learning: key to learning from experience. *Journal of Humanistic Psychology*, 23(2): 99–117.

Butler, D, Novak, H, Jarvis-Selinger, S and Beckingham, B (2004) Collaboration and self-regulation in teachers' professional development. *Teaching and Teacher Education,* 20: 435–55.

Clutterbuck, D (2004) *Everyone needs a mentor*. London: CIPD.

Cunliffe, A (2004) On becoming a critically reflexive practitioner. *Journal of Management Education*, 28(4): 407–26.

Daloz, L (1999) *Mentor: guiding the journey of adult learners*. New York: Jossey-Bass.

Davies, L (2006) Towards a new professionalism in the further education sector. *CPD Week* (free weekly e-bulletin for learning leaders), October 2006.

Dewey, J (original publication: 1910; new edition: 1991) *How we think.* New York: Prometheus Books.

Garvey, R, Stokes, P and Megginson, D (2009) *Coaching and mentoring theory and practice.* London: Sage Publications.

Ghaye, T (2008) *Building the reflective healthcare organsiation.* Oxford: Blackwell Publishing.

Ghaye, T, Melander-Wikman, A, Kisare, M, Chambers, P, Berhman, U, Kostenius, C and Lillyman, S (2008) Participatory and appreciative action and reflection (PAAR) – democratising reflective practices. *Reflective Practice,* 9(4): 361–97.

Goodmans, J (1984) reflection and teacher education: a case study and theoretical analysis. *Interchanges*, 15: 9–26.

Gravells, J (2010) Mentoring in theory and practice, in Wallace, S (ed) *The Lifelong Learning sector: reflective reader.* Exeter: Learning Matters.

Hackett, S (2001) Educating for competency and reflective practice: fostering a conjoint approach in education and training. *Journal of Workplace Learning*, 13(3): 103–12.

Kennett, K (2006) *Reflective practice: an alternative to supervision?* Unpublished Master's degree dissertation. Sheffield Hallam University.

Lee (2006) *Towards a new professionalism in the further education sector*. **www.teachingexpertise. com/articles/towards-a-new-professionalism-in-the-further-education-sector-1395** (accessed January 2010).

Lifelong Learning UK (2009) *A guide to support the professional development of diploma teachers*. London: LLUK.

Marcos, J, Miguel, E and Tillema, H (2009) Teacher reflection on action: what is said (in research) and is done (in teaching). *Reflective Practice*, 10(2): 191–204.

McLellan, E (2004) How reflective is the academic essay? *Studies in Higher Education*, 29: 321–46.

Mezirow, J (1981) A critical theory of adult learning and education. *Adult Education Quarterly*, 32(1): 3–24.

Mezirow, J (1991) *Transformative dimensions of adult learning*. New York: Jossey-Bass.

Plato (undated) *Apology* 38a. Available: **www.friesian.com/apology.htm** (accessed November 2009).

Platzer, H, Blake, D and Ashford, D (2000) Barriers to learning from reflection: a study of the use of groupwork with post-registration nurses. *Journal of Advanced Nursing*, 31(5): 1001–8.

Raelin, J (2001) Public relations as the basis of learning. *Management Learning*. 32(1): 11–30.

Raeilin, J (2008) *Worked-based learning: bridging knowledge and action in the work place*. San Francisco: Jossey-Bass.

Redmond, B (2006) *Reflection in action*. Aldershot: Ashgate.

Rennie, D L (2006) Reflexivity and its radical form. *Journal of Contemporary Psychotherapy*, 37(1): 53–58.

Roffey-Barentsen, J and Malthouse, R (2009) *Reflective practice in the Lifelong Learning sector*. Exeter: Learning Matters.

Schön, D A (1991) *The reflective practitioner*. Hampshire: Arena Ashgate Publishing.

Tellema, H (2006) Constructing knowledge in professional conversations: the role of beliefs on knowledge and knowing. *Learning and Instruction*, 16(6). Available: **plato.stanford.edu/entries/socrates/** (accessed November 2009).

Professional skills for reading and writing

This section aims to support and increase your understanding of some of the conventions for undertaking academic writing and applying them to the text. It focuses on section headings and topic sentences.

1 Section headings

Section headings are useful 'signposts' to themed sections throughout the main body of the discussion text. They enable the reader to flow through from one related sub-topic to the next, without losing the overall thread. They also:

- indicate the main theme of the upcoming section;
- help the reader organise the article's ideas;
- provide a preview of what the whole article is leading up to;
- provide a transition between the last section and the next one, which has a new main idea;
- enable the reader to zoom in on specific sections of text.

Action: Review the text and consider the added value of the section headings to your reading and understanding of the text.

Imagine if they were removed: What difference would that make to your interaction with the text?

2 Topic sentences

A *topic sentence*, also known as a focus sentence, helps to organise the whole paragraph and will generally appear at, or near, the beginning of the paragraph. In the same way that the overarching thesis statement acts as the unifying force for the whole essay, so the topic sentence acts as the unifying force in the paragraph. Working in two directions simultaneously, it relates the paragraph to the main theme of the writing, thus acting as a signpost for the argument of the paper as a whole, but it also defines the scope of the paragraph itself.

Generally, a topic sentence is a statement that makes some sort of a claim in the context of the paragraph as a whole. The claim should then be expanded, described, or evidenced, giving reasons or examples to support it. This is when you are likely to refer to other sources of information and where referencing becomes very important.

If you read an article of some length, it should be possible to read only the first sentence from each paragraph to get the gist of the content and direction of the main arguments. Consider the following disaggregated paragraph from the text beginning with the topic sentence itself:

One function of our participation in reflective practice is that we begin to realise the distinction between what we say we believe (our espoused theory) and what we do (our theories-in-use). This first sentence identifies the claim that I will attempt to evidence in the rest of the paragraph.

Argyris (1999) suggests that effective learning is the consequence of developing congruence between the two positions. In this second sentence, I refer to a credible source of research in the field to explain the importance of the claim.

A challenge for the reflective process is to increase our awareness of this discrepancy to reveal our underlying theory-in-use. This sentence increases the reader's awareness of the context in which the claim is situated.

This can be achieved by asking critical questions about the extent to which our actual behaviour aligns with our espoused theory and to what degree our inner feelings, beliefs and values emerge through our actions and practice. The concluding sentence wraps up the paragraph by suggesting a practical way to achieve the goal stated in the topic sentence:

Action: Select a paragraph from the text and identify the topic sentence. Explain how it:
- makes a claim, or puts forward an argument;
- links directly to the thesis of the whole text;
- defines the scope and indicates the direction for the rest of the paragraph.

Discussion

The tasks which follow will help you to explore the relevance of what you have read here to your own professional experience and practice.

DISCUSSION TASK

Can you identify opportunities for personal and professional development including new roles, risk-taking and ways to stretch your abilities?

Write down, MindMap or draw ways in which you do, or could, participate in critically reflective practice activities.

DISCUSSION TASK

Can you identify the potential barriers for *you* to engage in reflective practice?

What do you believe are the origins or causes of them?

What would be the benefits for you of reflecting on your practice?

DISCUSSION TASK

Do your reflective practices lead to improvement in your work?

How do you *measure* the impact of your reflective practice?

What was the last thing that you actively changed as a consequence of your reflection?

DISCUSSION TASK

What *process* have you tried using to reflect on your practice?

Describe the structure.

Was anyone else involved?

What sort of written account or record do you keep?

Where would you place your current position on the reflective taxonomy (see Figure 7.1 on page 72) and why?

FURTHER READING FURTHER READING **FURTHER READING** FURTHER READING

Altrichter, H, Kemmis, S, McTaggart, R and Zuber-Skerritt, O (2002) The concept of action research. *The Learning Organisation*, 9(3): 125–31.

Bolton, G (2001) Reflective practice: writing and professional development. London: Paul Chapman Publishing.

Claxton, G (1999) *Wise up: the challenge of lifelong learning.* London: Bloomsbury.

Coghlan, D and Brannick, T (2004) *Doing action research in your own Organisation* (2nd edn). London: Sage.

Cunliffe, A (2004) On becoming a critically reflexive practitioner. *Journal of Management Education*. 28(4): 418–24. Detailed information about critically reflexive practice journal use.

Dearing, R (1997) *Report of the National Committee of Inquiry into Higher Education.* Hayes: NCIHE.

Etherington, K (2004) *Becoming a reflexive researcher*. London: Jessica Kingsley Publishers.

Gray, D (2007) Facilitating management learning: developing critical reflection through reflective tools.

Management Learning, 38(5). For a range of creative options to engage in critical reflection.

Gray, D (2009) *Doing research in the real world*. London: Sage.

Habermas, J (1974) *Theory and practice* (translated Viertel, J). London: Heinemann.

Johns, C (1994) Guided reflection, in Palmer, A, Burns, S and Bulman, C (eds) *Reflective practice in nursing*. Oxford: Blackwell Science.

Kemmis, S and McTaggart, R (eds) (1988) *The action research planner* (3rd edn). Geelong, Victoria: Deakin University Press.

Kline, N (1999) *Time to think.* London: Cassell Illustrated.

Leshem, S and Trafford, V (2006) Stories as mirrors: reflective practice in teaching and learning. *Reflective Practice*, 7(1).

Maher, A (2004) Learning outcomes in higher education: implications for curriculum design and student learning. *Journal of Hospitality, Leisure, Sport and Tourism Education*, 3(2): 46–54.

McCormick Davis, S (2005) Developing reflective practice in pre-service student teachers: what does art have to do with it? *Teacher Development*, 9(1): 9–19.

Moran, A and Dallat, J (1995) Promoting reflective practice in initial teacher training. *International Journal of Educational Management*, 9(5): 20–26.

Mountford, B and Rogers, L (1996) Using individual and group reflection in and on assessment as a tool for effective learning. *Journal of Advanced Nursing*, 24: 1127–34.

Philip, L (2006) Encouraging reflective practice amongst students: a direct assessment approach. *Planet.* No. 17.

Pollner, M (1991) Left of ethnomethodology: the rise and decline of radical reflexivity. *American Sociological Review*, 56: 370–80.

Race, P (2002) *Evidencing reflection: putting the 'w' into reflection.* Available: **escalate.ac.uk/ resources/reflection/** (accessed November 2009).

Warin, J, Maddock, M, Pell, A and Hargreaves, L (2006) Resolving identity dissonance through reflective and reflexive practice in teaching. *Reflective Practice*, 7(2).

Wittgenstein, L (1980) *Remarks on the philosophy of psychology*, vols 1 and 2. Oxford: Blackwell.

Access to college and university databases yields the most up-to-date research articles about reflective practice across all professions.

The Institute for Learning is the independent employer-led sector skills council responsible for the professional development of staff working in the UK LLS. It can be accessed at: **www.ifl.ac.uk**.

8
Belonging and collegiality: the college as a community of practice

The aims of this chapter are to provide:

- a discussion of the culture and arrangements that are common in workplaces, particularly in education in the LLS;
- encouragement to compare your own experiences with those presented by published researchers;
- an opporunity to identify the issues involved in working effectively with professional colleagues.

What to look for

- As you read, think about the ideas discussed and how these relate to your own workplace and working arrangements.
- Notice how references to publications by more than one author are set out a) within the text, and b) in the list of references which follows.
- Notice, too, how references to material found on websites are set out a) in the text, and b) in the list of references which follows.

Author details

Belinda Ferguson and Anne Strong have worked in teacher education in the LLS for a combined 17 years and have both taught in FE colleges and communities at a range of levels. They both currently work as Course Leaders for the pre-service and in-service Certificate in Education at Burton College.

Belonging and collegiality: the college as a community of practice

Belinda Ferguson and *Anne Strong*

Abstract

This paper considers the recognition of communities of practice and the role that they can play in creating a dynamic and supportive workplace. It reviews some of the literature published about this topic and considers its relevance to the LLS. It explores the position of the individual within a community of practice, including factors which enable them to develop an holistic approach to teaching and learning. Suggestions are proposed for making communities of practice work effectively.

Introduction

Being a teacher in the LLS will require a wide variety of skills. Teachers must be experts in the subject they are teaching, having the appropriate qualifications or experience. However, it is not enough to have subject knowledge; teachers are also required to learn and develop skills to help the students gain the knowledge required to achieve their goals. To do this, teachers need to understand the process of learning and motivation, and must therefore be prepared to continue to learn themselves. Moreover, in the LLS, as in other sectors of education, teachers can also find themselves having to use or acquire skills to deal with a range of administration tasks. Throughout these processes, teachers will find themselves communicating and working with colleagues, which may involve discussing issues, support-ing each other and improving their practice. Lave and Wenger (1991) identify this collegiate context as a *community of practice* which is important for support, encouragement, integra-tion and learning. Teachers will certainly need to be able to prioritise, organise, and reflect on their own performance as well as that of the students; share good practice; and identify improvements. All of these aspects of their role may be enhanced by a community of practice. The LLS has been subject to frequent change in recent years (Wallace and Gravells, 2007), and the teachers and teaching teams at the heart of the learning organisation need to adapt their practice and have a commitment to ongoing improvement, for example by being creative and taking risks (Wallace and Gravells, 2007). It is apparent, therefore, that teaching is not, or should not be, an individual process but a team effort with a commitment to high standards and continual improvement.

Communities of practice are not exclusive to the LLS, or indeed to education, but may be found in all areas of life. Most people will have been involved in them at different times. Research has been undertaken to examine how these communities work in education and what their role is in teaching. This paper will consider the findings of the research and discuss how it relates to individual teachers in the LLS. It will explore the benefits of commu-nities of practice and learning organisations as well as identifying situations where they are not effective. It will also examine the dual role that teachers have in being a subject expert and a professional educator. It will conclude with suggestions on how to work effectively and efficiently with colleagues to enhance the enjoyment and satisfaction of working in a busy and demanding sector.

What are communities of practice?

Wenger (online, undated) defines communities of practice as *groups of people who share a concern or passion for something they do and learn how to do it better as they interact regularly* (p1). They are formed by people with a common goal or interest, sharing ideas and experiences, seeking to improve practice or find resolutions to situations. Lave and Wenger carried out research, published in 1991, into learning at work, suggesting that communities of practice are formed where individuals working together have a desire to learn from shared experiences. Wenger (ibid) identifies the short-term benefits to members as: receiv-ing help with challenges; having access to expertise within the community; creating meaningful work; and having fun with colleagues. In the longer term, values such as perso-nal development and professional identity are established with a network of professional colleagues. Wenger (ibid) also argues that the organisation benefits by having a proactive and problem-solving workforce who, by sharing knowledge and resources, will save time and create a synergy across units. Innovative practice and new strategies where individuals keep up to date within their subject will be encouraged. It will ensure the retention of, and maybe strengthen, the talent within the organisation and community, as the individual members develop strategic capabilities.

So how does this relate to teaching? In education, particularly in the LLS, it is usual for teams to work together within a department teaching on a course or a number of similar courses. With a shared interest, these individuals can become a community of practice who may discuss their teaching experience and learner progress, debate issues, share good practice and resources and find solutions to problems. The benefits of working together in this way can be numerous. Fuller et al (2005), who undertook research into Lave and Wenger's work, identified that each individual will have skills that they can take to a community of practice, and, by celebrating the range of skills and diversity of knowledge, the community will be enhanced. Roles, responsibilities and tasks can be shared among the group, utilising the skills of each individual to the benefit of all, so forming a cohesive team. The development of the learning experience is ensured if the community is proactive and willing to learn. Interaction between members enables familiarity with each other's methods and ways of thinking, encouraging individuals to take effective responsibility. Avis et al (2002) point out that Lave and Wenger's explanation of communities of practice emphasises the importance of dialogue and the willingness to seek resolutions to problems. In other words, it is not enough just to discuss issues, but it is also important to drive forward solutions and improve practice.

The dynamics of these communities have also been analysed by Lave and Wenger (1991) and are explained by Avis et al (2002). Lave and Wenger suggest that a new member of staff will begin as a peripheral member of the community and, as they gain experience and begin to add value, will become a fully accepted member, provided they engage in full participation. However, Avis et al (2002) argue that a novice may have valuable skills and knowledge that could result in full participation at a much earlier stage. They also express concern that having a peripheral role can lead to *disempowerment and exclusion from full participation* (p37). Trainee teachers can find themselves in this position or can even be excluded from a community, particularly pre-service trainees who are undertaking their teaching placement in a college. Bathmaker and Avis (2005) report on the frustrations experienced by such trainees who felt isolated and disappointed by the culture in which they were training. The intense workload of practising teachers did not allow for opportunities for reflection and discussion which, as discussed earlier, Lave and Wenger (1991) believe to be important to the individuals and the organisation. The trainee teachers in Bathmaker and Avis' (2005) study reported that they tried to engage in reflection with the experienced teachers, but became aware that this could uncomfortably challenge them. This is unfortunate because, as Wallace and Gravells (2007) point out, individuals, as part of a learning organisation, can benefit from self-reflection, since this leads to analysis and continual growth. Similarly, Fuller et al (2005) suggest that existing members of a community of practice can learn by responding to questions from trainees or individuals with different experiences.

We have seen that communities of practice are commonly found in all workplaces and are effective in helping learning to take place, enabling members to make sense of situations that they may not otherwise be able to do (Fuller et al, 2005). They can, in essence, help practitioners become better teachers by providing an opportunity for sharing problems and finding a way forward (Avis et al, 2002). Individuals bring their own identities and skills which add value to the community. They may initially be involved on the periphery and only gain a fuller role at a later stage, or may become fully involved early on. Avis et al (ibid) describe the *collective intelligence* that evolves as the intelligence of members is pooled to the advantage of the community as a whole. However, the process of becoming a member can be gradual and sometimes difficult (Colley et al, 2007). Fuller et al (2005) suggest that individuals may need to *choose* to become a member and show a willingness to fit in, otherwise they can become marginalised.

Let us now consider whether communities of practice can work effectively in the LLS. The research discussed previously suggests that they can and the benefits are clearly identified. However, the exclusion or marginalisation of individuals as identified by Bathmaker and Avis (2005) and Fuller et al (2005) can certainly occur, as we have seen in the case of some student teachers. Indeed, there are many teachers in the LLS who have little contact with other members of staff. Often these individuals teach in the evenings, or work in the community, at satellite centres or in company workplaces, for example, and will have little opportunity to engage with their colleagues. Many teachers in this sector work part-time, often for more than one organisation, and can experience conflict between them. This can mean that instead of being a member of more than one community, the teacher is on the periphery of them all and consequently experiencing a feeling of not belonging to any.

Some teachers may feel that they do not fit into a team and will not benefit from the shared experiences. Even colleagues who do work together may actually find it difficult to meet. The heavy workload, different timetables and no common meeting point can restrict opportunities for such interaction. As Bathmaker and Avis (2005) pointed out, trainee teachers can find that frustrations over the lack of resources, workspace and access to photocopiers add to the feeling of marginalisation. This can also be true of part-time or new members of staff; and so the individual who may benefit the most from being part of a community of practice can be excluded from doing so. However, it should also be noted that communities of practice do not always offer the appropriate support to their members. Issues can become insular and internalised, but a broader perspective may be required to increase understanding. Colley et al (2007) discuss how individuals may benefit from seeking reassurance or guidance from a wider community, but found that this can lead to some degree of exclusion from their local one.

Making it work

The value of communities of practice has been considered, as have the drawbacks. So, how can they best be made to work? Recognition of the value of communities of practice must be the first stage, followed by a conscious decision to be involved and a willingness to contribute and learn. Wenger (online, undated) gives some useful suggestions as to how to cultivate a community where one does not currently exist or does not operate effectively. A strategic context needs to be set, which legitimises the practice. This approach would necessitate involving the individuals who may have been excluded and identifying a way to include them. Such solutions would go some way to ensuring that part-time staff have adequate resources, including a desk and computer access, which reinforces a sense of belonging; arranging meetings and staff development sessions at mutually convenient times; and recognising the diversity of skills within the community in order to use them to the best advantage. Wenger (ibid) suggests that individuals and management need to be educated so that they can understand how the communities could work and are given support to enable this CPD to take place. This may include technology to ensure that peripatetic staff can still communicate with their colleagues.

However, it has to be realised that communities will take time to become fully effective. Wenger (ibid) further proposes that pilot projects can assist in the development of the culture and that successes must be publicised to show the value of the community to aid full integration into the organisation. It is important to recognise that communities will be affected by staff turnover and, as jobs or roles change, so will the identities within the community (Fuller et al, 2005). It should also be acknowledged that staff restructuring can affect existing communities but may also provide an opportunity to create new ones. Staff working in more than one area or organisation should be encouraged to share the good practice with both to allow a cross-fertilisation of ideas. This also helps members of the communities to see a bigger picture of the organisation rather than being limited within their own area.

Communities of practice can, sometimes, evolve naturally and without conscious intent; but in a busy sector with a variety of working arrangements, they may need to be cultivated. A leader will usually be required to encourage contribution from all members. Where they do or could exist, individuals should embrace the support that they can offer and welcome the sharing of expertise, resources and opportunities created so that learning and personal development can take place. A community that is close knit but not closed (Fuller et al, 2005) will be effective in achieving this.

Becoming a professional educator

Individuals joining the LLS may come from previous communities of practice, such as university, industry or other organisations, and may find the sector to be quite unusual with different pressures from those expected or previously encountered. Moving from one community or, indeed, industry to another can be a challenging process. A four-year study, 'Transforming Learning Cultures in Further Education', which ended in 2005 encountered teachers who described themselves as *accidental tutors* who identified more closely with their former profession (Colley et al, 2007). This illustrates the difficulty that some individuals have in the transition from a vocational expert to a professional educator. A change in attitude and behaviour is often required to facilitate this. The teacher may need to consider, for example, their dress code and decide what is appropriate for the environment within which they now work. The type of language they use may need to be modified to ensure that it is appropriate for the level of learners and ensures their respect. While teachers need to remain up to date with the skills of their vocation or knowledge of their subject, they must also be prepared to learn new skills and ideas to enable them to undertake the role of a teacher, or what is often described as a *learning facilitator* (Avis et al, 2002). One such skill is being able to transfer knowledge and skills into the appropriate context for the learners. Consider a very experienced and qualified construction worker who is asked to deliver a unit on construction safety as part of a health and safety professional qualification. This teacher will need to transfer their knowledge of the subject and express it, not from the perspective of a construction worker, but from that of a health and safety professional who will have a different focus. This requires an understanding of the learners, familiarity with the syllabus from which they are working and an awareness of how they will be assessed. It is a complex task and requires skills not easily acquired.

Conclusion

A successful community of practice will continually develop a teacher's professional skills. The benefits to a new teacher, who has participated in a comprehensive induction programme to the organisation's wider community, are the provision of local support and guidance. In the case of the construction worker above, the community of practice can aid in their transfer of knowledge from one perspective to another. Within a community of practice, an ethos of welcoming new people and offering mutual support will ensure that teachers and learners alike benefit from a developing team. However, it is important to recognise that the personal and group gain from the community will only be achieved if participants are willing to contribute and learn. This requires a keen desire to share information and find solutions to problems. Colleagues who can benefit the most from the support available are often those who have difficulty accessing it, and so arrangements to ensure that the community is available for all may need to be established and maintained to ensure their successful contribution to CPD.

References

Avis, J, Bathmaker, A and Parsons, J (2002) Communities of practice and the construction of learners in post-compulsory education and training. *Journal of Vocational Education and Training*, 54(1): 27–50.

Bathmaker, A and Avis, J (2005) Becoming a lecturer in further education in England: the construction of professional identity and the role of communities of practice. *Journal of Education for Teaching,* 31(1): 47–62.

Colley, H, James, D, Diment, K (2007) Unbecoming teachers: towards a more dynamic notion of professional participation. *Journal of Education Policy*, 22(2): 173–93.

Fuller, A, Hodkinson, H, Hodkinson, P and Unwin, L (2005) Learning as peripheral participation in communities of practice: a reassessment of key concepts in workplace learning. *British Educational Journal*, 31(1): 49–68.

Lave, J and Wenger, E (1991) *Situated learning.* Cambridge: Cambridge University Press.

Wallace, S and Gravells, J (2007) *Mentoring* (2nd edn). Exeter: Learning Matters.

Wenger, E (undated) *Cultivating communities of practice.* Available: **www.ewenger.com** (accessed November 2009).

Professional skills for reading and writing

This section aims to highlight some of the conventions of formal academic writing. It looks at the citing of publications by multiple authors and at referencing to websites.

1 Multiple authors

You will have noticed in the paper that the writers make several references to publications which have more than one author. Where a publication has two authors, both names are cited. Some examples in this paper are: Wallace and Gravells (2007); Lave and Wenger (1991); Bathmaker and Avis (2005).

However, when a book or paper has more than two authors it is usual practice to give the name of the first-named author, followed by *et al*, which is a Latin phrase meaning *and all the rest*. Examples in this paper include Fuller et al (2005) and Colley et al (2007). In the list of references which follow the paper, the list of authors is conveyed to the reader in full (in these two cases, *Fuller, A, Hodkinson, H, Hodkinson, P and Unwin, L (2005);* and *Colley, H, James, D and Diment, K (2002)*).

2 Referencing to websites

The writers of this paper refer several times to work by Wenger which they have accessed on a website. Notice that they have referenced this in the text by indicating that they are referring to work found online. When listing this reference at the end of the paper they have given the website address and the date on which the material referred to was accessed. This is accepted practice. It is important because websites can appear and disappear, and their content can change, sometimes from day to day. The *date it was accessed*, therefore, is crucial for the sake of accuracy. You will also note that in this instance *no date of publication* can be given, presumably because the website did not provide this information. This is often the case with text accessed on websites. The term to use in this case is: *undated.*

Discussion

The discussion topics which follow will help you to review and consider what you have read, and to analyse it in relation to your own situation.

DISCUSSION TASK

According to this paper, what factors contribute towards making a successful community of practice?

DISCUSSION TASK

What indications can you find in the paper that there could be times when a community of practice might not provide appropriate support to its members?

DISCUSSION TASK

Are you able to identify the community of practice within which you work? In thinking about this you might find it useful to consider the following.

● It may be that you work within more than one.

● An open plan arrangement within a staffroom may enable you to participate in supportive activities with people from other subject areas.

● You may have undertaken your training with people employed in other organisations.

● The area of learning in which you work may be arranged in such a way that you are able to share ideas with people who teach a different range of students to you.

FURTHER READING FURTHER READING **FURTHER READING** FURTHER READING

Barton, D and Tusting, K (eds) (2005) *Beyond communities of practice: language, power and social context*. Cambridge: Cambridge University Press.

Hildreth, PM and Kimble C (eds) (2004) *Knowledge networks: innovation through communities of practice*. London: Idea Group Publishing.

Wenger, E (1999) *Communities of practice: learning, meaning and identity*. Cambridge: Cambridge University Press.

9
Mentoring in theory and practice

The aims of this chapter are to provide:

- an example of academic writing style;
- a template for structuring a piece of academic writing;
- an exploration of some of the research to date relating to the challenges of mentoring within a Lifelong Learning context;
- an opportunity to relate these ideas to your own practical experience and observations about mentoring, either as mentor or mentee;
- an opportunity to expand your understanding of academic vocabulary;
- a demonstration of how information for various sources can be synthesised to create clear learning outcomes.

What to look for

- As you read through this chapter make a note of any unfamiliar words or phrases that you come across.
- Look at how the author summarises and combines information from different sources. What methods are used to do this?

Author details

Jonathan Gravells is an independent consultant who spent many years as a Human Resources Director in private industry. He now spends a lot of his time mentoring and coaching individuals in both the public and the private sector, as well as training mentors and helping organisations set up mentoring schemes. He has published books and articles on mentoring, leadership and change, many dealing specifically with the LLS.

Mentoring in theory and practice

Jonathan Gravells

Abstract

This paper examines the proven benefits of mentoring for staff development in the education sector, as well as some of the harmful outcomes which can occur, using as evidence a recent review of research on beginning teachers. It supports these findings by reference to previous mentoring research in a much wider context, and suggests some hypotheses as to what factors may determine the likelihood of either successful or damaging outcomes from mentoring in the LLS. Specifically it outlines four of the key challenges facing individuals and institutions in trying to make mentoring work: definition of the mentoring role, conditions for mentoring, relationship quality and matters of technique. Using well-established mentoring theories and more recent research, the paper argues that reaping the benefits of this kind of learning dialogue depends very much on how individuals and organisations respond to these four challenges.

Introduction

Over the last thirty years mentoring has developed in schools, colleges, industry and commerce as an increasingly popular way of supporting the learning of students, new employees, trainees and experienced staff. Its growing popularity has been based on a perception that, as a developmental process, it offers the various participants benefits above and beyond those of other approaches to learning. A recent examination of existing research, specifically in the context of the educational environment, confirmed the following benefits accruing to the mentee, the mentor and the wider institution.

Benefits for the mentee include:

- reduced feelings of isolation;
- better adaptation to norms and expectations of institution and profession as a whole;
- increased confidence and self-esteem;
- professional growth;
- improved behaviour and classroom management skills;
- improved time management;
- improved self-reflection and problem-solving capacities;
- perspective on difficult experiences;
- increased morale and job satisfaction.

Benefits for the mentor include:

- positive impact on personal and professional development;
- improved ability to learn through self-reflection on own practice;
- opportunity to talk to others about teaching and learning;
- new and improved teaching styles;
- improved communication skills;
- satisfaction and pride in helping others succeed;
- enhanced career planning through identifying own priorities.

Benefits for the organisation include:

- increased staff retention and stability;
- staff getting to know each other better;
- increased collaboration;
- more developed culture of professional development;
- more cost-effective training and development of staff.

(Hobson et al, 2009).

The various functions of mentoring, both career and psychosocial, were extensively examined by Kram (1985). Career outcomes, factors that enhance career advancement, would include such things as challenging assignments, exposure to new experiences and skills development, whereas psychosocial outcomes would include having a role model, counselling and support. To these two categories Gibb (1984) helpfully adds learning as a third set of outcomes, and later researchers have concentrated on accessing tacit knowledge and observational learning (Noe, 1988; Ibarra, 2000). So while Hobson et al's (2009) review focuses particularly on work with beginning teachers, the research seems to confirm many of the same benefits of mentoring that have been identified in a much wider context.

Yet, we know also that mentoring can frequently result either in such benefits not being fully realised, or even in mentees, mentors and organisations reporting negative consequences. Examples of these might include:

- fostering elitism;
- excluding the socially different;
- 'cloning' people;
- destroying self-confidence;
- suppressing innovation and supporting the status quo;
- undermining autonomy and creating dependent learners;
- manipulating and bullying learners.

(Scandura, 1998; Feldman, 1999; Eby et al, 2004).

Once again, such themes in the wider mentoring world seem to be reflected in the education sector as well. Hobson et al (2009) found significant evidence of how this *dark side of mentoring* (Long, 1997) can also affect the different parties.

Effects on the mentee include:

- unavailability of and insufficient support for mentee's emotional and psychological well-being;
- increased pressure and anxiety;
- feeling bullied;
- not being sufficiently challenged;
- not given enough responsibility or freedom to innovate;
- a focus on technical skills development at the expense of broader self-directed learning skills, such as critical reflection.

Effects on the mentor include:

- increased workload;
- feelings of insecurity, threat or inadequacy;
- a sense of isolation.

Effects on the organisation include:

- staff withdrawing from the training or even profession;
- an increase in 'theory–practice dualism' and poor application of theoretical concepts;
- the promotion of conventional as opposed to innovative practices;
- a lack of challenge and reform.

(Hobson et al, 2009)

So why is it that individuals' experience of mentoring can vary so widely, and what factors seem to have most impact upon the likelihood of institutions deriving the maximum benefit from mentoring and avoiding its potential pitfalls? The answers may be grouped under four key headings: definition of role, conditions for mentoring, relationship quality and mentoring technique.

Definition of role

For some, many aspects of the continuing debate about differences between the roles of mentor and coach have become increasingly tedious and even irrelevant, as terms like coaching and mentoring become used more and more interchangeably. Certainly, as the practice of such learning partnerships develops and matures, mentoring and coaching would seem to have far more characteristics in common than distinctions. Depending on context both may:

- be more or less directive;
- draw upon the coach/mentor's experience;
- last varying amounts of time;
- involve goals emanating from the learner and others;
- address both skills and knowledge development as well as 'life transitions' and broader personal growth agendas.

(Clutterbuck, 2008)

It is also true to say that for almost every dogmatic list of distinctions between roles one can find another equally confident assertion that contradicts it, and favoured definitions, even just within the education sector, will vary. However, when we widen the range of roles to include teacher, instructor and assessor, it is impossible to avoid the need for clarity of terminology. Without wishing to add to an already conflicting array of definitions, it is important for us at least to consider what it is that characterises mentoring as a role and a process, and examine how some of the differences in perception may affect learning outcomes.

Some of the differences in perception may emanate from a long-established distinction traditionally separating European and US schools of thought. In the US mentoring has by and large developed along a sponsorship model, with 'protégés' (their preferred term for 'mentees') benefiting from the wise counsel of older and more experienced mentors. The relationship is defined by the power and influence of the mentor. By contrast, the prevailing paradigm in Europe is one of developmental mentoring, in which the focus is on the mentee's agenda, and the emphasis is on mutual learning and helping the mentee to do things for themselves. This is achieved not just by helping them to learn new ideas, perspectives and skills, but also by helping them to learn how to learn (Clutterbuck, 2008). It is also worth pointing out that the geographical split, while convenient, may be over-simplistic. Laurent Daloz, for example, an American academic concerned with mentoring specifically in adult education, writes of mentors fighting their desire to teach and change the mentee (Daloz, 1999). Under the developmental model, a mentee is ideally left more autonomous, independent and better able to make meaning of, and derive learning from, their own experiences, without external help. These differences in schools of thought on either side of the Atlantic also mean that US-based research into mentoring (including Kram (1985) and others cited above) has to be read with such underpinnings in mind. Of course, many mentoring roles do not fall neatly into one or other of these camps. They may be an amalgam of different aspects. Nevertheless, as one criterion for assessing how the mentoring role is portrayed in your institution, the two models may be helpful, not least because from them spring a number of other contingent characteristics of the role.

The power relationship, for example, is very clearly defined and overt in sponsorship mentoring. The mentor is presented as someone more experienced, qualified and able, to whom the mentee should defer, and whose advice and guidance they should follow. While it would be untrue to say that developmental mentors are not more senior and experienced (they very often are), the underlying premise is that different, as well as greater, experience and expertise can be every bit as helpful. Both parties can benefit from the other's perspective. Any power difference is there to be played down and overcome in favour of a mutual learning model where challenging and questioning by the mentee is not only accepted but actively encouraged.

It follows from this that the sponsorship mentor role is at least partly there to impart knowledge and skill, and therefore 'telling' or 'advising' has equal status with questioning and challenging in the way these mentors relate to their learners. Conversely, the developmental school of mentoring would assert that the primary focus of the role should be on questioning the learner, encouraging them to reflect on their experience and generate solutions and outcomes for themselves which are compatible with their own personality and style. Only as a last resort would a developmental mentor adopt an information-giving role, and even then it would more likely, in the first instance, take the form of signposting or sharing experience with the mentee's permission, rather than imposing ideas and solutions.

While both of these extremes might result in mentees improving their technical skills and knowledge, the sponsorship role is less likely to result in the mentee developing independent learning skills. On the other hand, the developmental mentor role, at its best, concentrates on helping the mentee reflect on and analyse their experiences in order to become a more effective and autonomous learner. This hopefully generates increased self-reliance and independence of thought on the part of the mentee, and, from the organisation's perspective, is more likely to result in what Chris Argyris (1990) refers to as *double-loop learning*. It is perhaps an over-simplification, but where sponsorship mentoring tends to favour consistency and consolidation of the status quo, developmental mentoring should encourage challenge to existing assumptions and, by extension, greater innovation.

The dimensions of the two role definitions are summarised in Table 9.1 on page 95.

I have heard the view expressed that many experienced teachers strongly resent the idea of being 'mentored', but are more amenable to the prospect of being 'coached'. Could this be an indication that, in their school or college, the role of mentoring is seen as telling inexperienced staff how to do their job better (i.e. incorporating many characteristics of the sponsorship model)? It is not difficult to see how a lack of clarity about the mentor's role, or even a cynical gulf between the 'espoused' model and the reality of its application, might result in damaging effects such as:

- suppressing innovation;
- creating dependent learners;
- feelings of inadequacy;
- a focus on technical skills.

Conditions for mentoring

The way we define the role of mentor, and especially the conflicts arising from this definition, or lack of it, will have a knock-on effect on the conditions for mentoring within the institution. For example, a perception of mentoring as primarily a means of experienced teachers passing on technical expertise to new recruits is likely to result in a more formalised

Table 9.1 Characteristics of mentoring role

Sponsorship mentoring	Developmental mentoring
Power is with more senior, experienced and knowledgeable mentor	Mentor need not have greater experience or knowledge, only different. Power is 'parked'
Mentor's role is to provide protection and promotion, but also to impart skills and knowledge	Mentor's role is to support and encourage, but primarily to question and challenge mentee in order to help them generate their own insights
Little or no emphasis on learning to learn	Primary emphasis on learning to learn
More likely to result in dependency	More likely to result in autonomy and independent thinking
Mentee agenda subservient to that of organisation?	Mentee encouraged to challenge organisational norms and assumptions

scheme, where the aims of the mentoring, as well as the control, monitoring and evaluation are all controlled by the institution. It will tend, furthermore, to be integrated with external standards, competencies and targets, since the development of new staff is subject to such national frameworks and indeed will be assessed against these. Inevitably, the agenda for mentoring, under these circumstances, will be at least in part determined from outside, rather than by the individual learner, and the role of the mentor will often encompass assessment (for example, via classroom observation) in addition to learning support. Given such an emphasis on consistency in meeting standards, it may also follow that mentoring in such circumstances is a compulsory part of CPD.

At the opposite extreme, an organisation might view mentoring as an additional personal and career development facility available to any member of staff who cares to take advantage of it, at whatever stage in their career, and the impetus for which must come entirely from the individual. The kind of conditions here might be very different. The institution may interfere little in relationships. Not only the driving force for the relationship, but the very task of setting it up in the first instance, will lie squarely with the learner. The development agenda will be largely or even entirely their own, and may or may not correspond to national standards, and the mentor will play no part in assessing the learner, only in enabling them to reflect on their own performance.

Neither set of conditions is wholly good or wholly bad, and nor are any of the myriad combinations in between. But they will lead to different experiences on the part of mentors and mentees, and affect the likelihood of both the desirable and undesirable outcomes of the mentoring process that have been outlined already. Some time ago now research indicated that mentoring tended to produce better outcomes when it took place in a more informal context (Ragins and Cotton, 1999), a view that has been taken up by others (Garvey and Alred, 2000). The idea here is that in informal schemes mentors are better motivated, the process focuses more on the learner's long-term needs, and mentors are seen as more effective. However, to conclude from this that informal is 'better' ignores the advantages that a degree of structure and formality can have in providing clear purpose, proper support frameworks for participants, quality training, and in mitigating against the risks of poorly executed mentoring by inexpert, or even 'toxic' mentors (Ehrich and Hansford, 1999). Without a degree of formality, some groups might find themselves denied the benefits of mentoring altogether. Long (1997) highlighted the fact that often those chosen to be mentors were already managing a heavy workload and struggled to accommodate the additional demands of mentoring others. Certainly, many mentors in the teaching profession will recognise this dilemma. While some formal schemes will ensure separate allocation of time, and even additional rewards, formalisation by no means guarantees this. One possible conclusion to draw from this slightly conflicting evidence is that conditions for mentoring can include both 'helpful' support mechanisms, and less 'helpful' controls. In other words, where formality is about providing high quality training, allocating dedicated time and giving continuing support to mentors and mentees, the impact is likely to be positive. Where formality is more about the institution expecting automatic compliance from staff while exercising control over everything from individual development agendas to who your mentor is, the potential for negative experiences may be higher.

In a similar way, previous research has suggested that voluntary participation in mentoring, by both parties, produces more positive outcomes than situations where the mentoring entails an element of compulsion (Cunningham, 1993; Ehrich and Hansford, 1999). Formality and a degree of compulsion often go hand in hand. However, a formal mentoring scheme can have voluntary arrangements (i.e. where mentors and mentees get to choose whether they participate or not, and who they pair up with). This provides equality of opportunity, but the concern of the institution may be once again about how they ensure common standards and equal participation without some element of compulsion. While evidence to date indicates that mentoring relationships where the parties have some say in the pairing can produce better quality outcomes, complete freedom of choice can also result in undemanding partnerships. As a result, some have recommended a form of 'guided choice', where mentees may choose their mentor from a shortlist provided by the organisation (Clutterbuck, 1991). Combining some of these research findings allows us to summarise the impact different conditions might have on the likely outcomes of mentoring (see Table 9.2).

Relationship quality

What is striking as we examine the influence of role definition and conditions for mentoring is how much of the potential for benefit or harm centres around the quality of the relationship itself. A common factor across many of the variables mentioned so far (power dynamics in the relationship, the balance of instruction versus self-directed learning, mentee autonomy, enforcement of structures and agendas, and the conflation of mentoring and assessment) is that the trust and rapport vital to an intense learning partnership can be undermined and diluted. We cannot have it both ways. The price we must pay, it seems, for the privilege of closely controlling mentoring, imposing standard processes and agendas, and providing an element of assessment and instruction is often a weakening of the bond between mentor and mentee.

To what extent should we be concerned about this? Well, there is pretty compelling evidence to suggest that the quality of the mentoring relationship may actually be the single most critical factor in determining mentee attitudes towards job and career (Ragins,

Table 9.2 Mentoring: impact of different conditions

Conditions	Advantages	Disadvantages
Completely informal	Responsibility with learner Improved self-reliance and independent learning Focus on mentee needs Mentor more motivated	Lack of overall purpose Little or no training Incompetent mentors Poor support networks No resources allocated Some people excluded
'Benign' formality	Good quality training Allocation of time and resources Continuing support for mentees and mentors Reduced isolation and feelings of insecurity Clear purpose for institution Equal opportunity	Some responsibility and intitiative removed from mentee
'Institutional' formality	Some or all of above, plus closer control of process, mentor allocation, and learning agenda	Less freedom to question and innovate Less emphasis on personal growth and learning to learn Equal access may suffer Time allocation may be squeezed
Voluntary	Better motivated partnerships Rapport built quickly Encourages independence	No control over pairings Unequal participation Common aims and standards very difficult
Compulsory	Standard provision Equal participation Fair to all More control of pairings	Feelings of pressure and inadequacy more likely Reinforces status quo
Imposed standards	Common treatment and assessment for all Learners know what to expect	Learners sacrifice some or all of own agenda to blanket standards and targets Learners less committed
Mentor also expected to assess	Mentor can give detailed feedback to reinforce learning agenda Mentee is challenged	Trust in learning partnership undermined by suspicion and insecurity Mentee may become reliant on feedback at expense of critical self-reflection

Cotton and Miller, 2000). Even more than factors such as formality of programmes or involvement in matching, perceived relationship quality seems to affect mentee satisfaction, to the extent that even non-mentored individuals report better attitudes to mentoring than those in 'poor' relationships. Such evidence raises some interesting questions to be addressed in evaluating the mentoring schemes in our own institutions. To what extent is the overwhelming importance of relationship quality reflected in:

- the initial training given to mentors and mentees;
- the continuing development and supervision of mentors;
- the evaluation of the mentoring programme;
- the way mentors and mentees are matched;
- the additional demands made on mentors which may conflict with an open, trusting and non-judgemental relationship (for example, assessment, line management, etc.)?

For example, are we still treating rapport-building as a relatively superficial social exchange of biographical information, or as a deep understanding of each other's values, beliefs and dreams, based on what might occasionally be uncomfortable and awkward questions and self-disclosure? Do we see trust and rapport as the result of an expertly applied series of 'interpersonal techniques' or as contingent on a much less formulaic process of earning and demonstrating trust and respect through authenticity, integrity and real caring for the well-being of the other party (Wallace and Gravells, 2007a)? I am hardly alone in arguing that to produce the kind of insight and learning achieved by the very best mentoring relationships, mentors need an understanding of what makes their mentee 'tick' that goes well beyond the concept of rapport implied by 'normal', social intercourse. But I would further assert that this is still greatly underestimated by many institutions, scheme organisers and mentors. If the research suggests that some mentees can feel unsupported emotionally and psychologi-cally, or even, in some cases, bullied, it seems likely that the quality of the relationship is playing some significant part in this outcome.

Mentoring technique

Having examined how the definition of the mentor's role, the conditions under which mentoring takes place and the quality of the mentoring relationship can all play a part in determining successful development outcomes or otherwise, this paper finally turns its attention to the detail of how mentoring is actually practised. Potentially a massive topic in its own right, the intention here is to focus on four specific areas: **goal-setting, challenge and support, sharing knowledge** and **degree of intervention**.

Recent research by Megginson and Clutterbuck has questioned the widely accepted ortho-doxy that successful outcomes in learning relationships are positively correlated with **clear and specific goals** early on. For many years, a consistent thrust in mentoring and coaching literature, and indeed leadership and management manuals, has been that specific, measur-able, agreed, realistic and time-bound (SMART) objectives offer the best chance of achieving the desired outcome. Recent studies of mentoring pairs has indicated that, in fact, the more specific the goal at the beginning of the relationship, the less likely it is to lead to success (Clutterbuck, 2008). (Interestingly, the same research also identified quality of relationship as the single greatest determinant of success – see section above.) It would appear that the effect of goals, what we mean by the term, and how we use them in mentoring partnerships is rather more complex than previously thought. Too close a focus on objectives early on in a learning dialogue can limit discussion and fails to take account of the often emergent nature of goals. Such specificity early on can result in a headlong dash towards narrowly defined measures of success, without gaining a broader understanding and appreciation of the mentee's personal context, values, beliefs and longer-term dreams. It also disregards the influence that uncertainty, randomness and accident can have on our learning. Management self-help manuals are fond of citing Kennedy's goal of putting a man on the moon as an example of the power of goals. However true this may be, it conveniently ignores the many strides forward in human knowledge that have resulted from chance events and accidental associations. What lessons does this hold for practising mentors? Well, it reinforces the need for them to review regularly the mentee's individual goals and the objectives of the relationship (Hobson et al, 2009). It also raises some challenging questions about the efficacy of goals that are exclusively focused on externally imposed national standards – a feature of many mentoring partnerships in Lifelong Learning and the education sector in general. But, more than this, it suggests that a more gradual and iterative approach to goal-setting might serve mentors and mentees better. I offer one version of what this might look like in Figure 9.1.

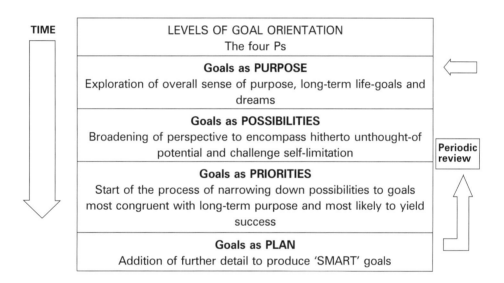

Figure 9.1 Levels of goal orientation

One of the negative outcomes of mentoring uncovered by Hobson et al's (2009) review of the research on beginning teachers was an insufficient **amount of challenge** by mentors, manifesting itself particularly in such symptoms as an over-cautious approach to giving responsibility and the lack of freedom to innovate. Significantly, evidence also emerged from this review of some mentees reporting a lack of psychological and emotional support. The way in which mentors combine their twin roles of support and challenge would therefore appear to be highly pertinent to the achievement of positive outcomes. Indeed, a strong emphasis on both activities in the mentoring process was advocated in the context of adult education some time ago (Daloz, 1999). Daloz saw challenge and support as twin pillars essential in promoting feelings of trust and agency. We all know instinctively that we will tolerate far greater degrees of challenge from someone who we feel is supportive, wants us to succeed and has our interests at heart. High levels of challenge combined with high levels of support are most likely to promote growth. Support alone may feel very therapeutic and affirming, but is unlikely to lead to learning in the long term, and unrelieved challenge without any sense of support will tend to generate defensiveness and feelings of inadequacy (Wallace and Gravells, 2007b).

Another aspect of mentoring technique which has an impact on the likelihood of negative or positive outcomes is the way in which **experience and knowledge is shared**. As indicated above, a view of the mentoring role which emphasises the transmission of expertise from the 'older and wiser' mentor to the grateful mentee is likely to encourage a more didactic, instructional and directive approach. It is not difficult to see how this might result in dependency and lack of innovation. One might argue, furthermore, that an insistence on combining mentoring and assessment roles, and on imposing learning agendas based entirely on external standards and targets will conspire to exacerbate this tendency. Moreover, in an education context many mentors are adjusting to a mentoring role from a teaching role which may have been much more directive and instructional. All of this suggests that mentors in Lifelong Learning may want to give particular attention to this aspect of their practice. No one is suggesting that there is no place in mentoring for advice or straight answers. If a mentor is dealing with a situation where there is clearly a right and wrong answer (for example, a new teacher wants to know the college convention on lesson plans), the most helpful response would be to provide the information. However, the nature of learning agendas in most mentoring partnerships makes such matters of fact the exception rather than the rule. So, when addressing matters of opinion, judgement, personal style, etc., such as how to deal with disruptive student behaviour, we are dealing with problems that have multiple answers. In these circumstances, the way a mentor responds will influence both the mentee's short-term ability to deal with the issue and their long-term ability to resolve such challenges for themselves. Our natural instinct may be to 'rescue' the mentee, either because this is what feels instinctively most helpful, or because, as teacher/manager/parent, we have become conditioned to seeing our role as one of providing solutions and imparting wisdom. Yet we also know that finding our own solutions results in greater satisfaction, better recall, more effective synthesis of theory and practice, and better exercise of that critical self-reflection muscle that will reduce our dependence on mentors coaches or teachers. What do you do?

If we see the sharing of experience and the offering of advice as an acceptable last resort, a formula from the world of coaching may prove helpful. Myles Downey suggests a number of precautions.

- Always OFFER advice/idea – only give it if accepted.
- Try to give learner some CHOICE.
- Immediately return to non-directive mode.
- Be transparent about your intention – 'I have some experience that might be instructive here. Do you want me to share it?'

(Adapted from Downey, 2003)

Finally, I would encourage practising mentors to reflect upon the **balance between intervention and passive forms of support** in their mentoring style.

Challenging questions, insightful reflecting back, role-play, models, action planning and feedback can all play a part in a productive mentoring partnership. But we should not allow prior conditioning about what feels helpful to us to make us badger learners with unwanted and unproductive interventions. Listening, empathising, holding emotions, maintaining ambiguity, and allowing learners to struggle also contribute to effective outcomes.

We all need the opportunity sometimes to rehearse our own arguments on a topic and arrive at our own reasoning, and the most useful gift from our mentor at this point may be silence. The balance will depend upon the needs of the mentee at the time, and will require the mentor to be sensitive to what these are. An over-emphasis on intervention may deprive the learner of the opportunity to wonder, reflect, make mistakes and experiment with their own intrinsic knowledge, all of which may make the difference between satisfaction, a sense of autonomy, and personal growth and learning, or demotivation dependency, and a lack of challenge.

References

Argyris, C (1990) *Overcoming organisational defences: facilitating organisational learning*. Needham, MA: Allyn & Bacon.

Clutterbuck, D (1991) *Everyone needs a mentor* (2nd edn). London: CIPD.

Clutterbuck, D (2008) What's happening in coaching and mentoring? And what is the difference between them? *Development and Learning in Organisations*, 22(4): 8–10.

Cunningham, J (1993) Facilitating a mentorship programme, *Leadership and Organisational Development Journal*, 14(4): 15–20.

Daloz, L (1999) *Mentor: guiding the journey of adult learners*. San Francisco: Jossey-Bass.

Downey, M (2003) *Effective coaching* (2nd edn). US: Texere Publishing.

Eby, L, Butts, M, Lockwood, A and Shana, S (2004) Proteges' negative mentoring experiences, *Personnel Psychology*, 57(2): 411–47.

Ehrich, L and Hansford, B (1999) Mentoring: pros and cons for HRM. *Asia Pacific Journal of Human Resources*, 37: 92–107.

Feldman, D (1999) Toxic mentors or toxic protégés? A critical re-examination of dysfunctional mentoring. *Human Resource Management Review*, 9(3): 247.

Garvey, B and Alred, G (2000) Developing mentors. *Career Development International*, 5(4/5): 216–22.

Gibb, S (1994) Evaluating mentoring. *Education + Training*, 36(5): 32–9.

Hobson, A, Ashby, P, Malderez, A and Tomlinson, P (2009) Mentoring beginning teachers: what we know and what we don't. *Teaching and Teacher Education*, 25: 207–16.

Ibarra, H (2000) Making partner: a mentor's guide to the psychological journey. *Harvard Business Review*, 78(2): 146–55.

Kram, K (1985) *Mentoring at work*. Boston: Scott, Foresman & Company.

Long, J (1997) The dark side of mentoring. *Australian Educational Researcher*, 24(2): 115–33.

Noe, R (1988) An investigation of the determinants of successful assigned mentoring relationships. *Personnel Psychology*, 41(3): 457–79.

Ragins, B and Cotton, J (1999) Mentor functions and outcomes: a comparison of men and women in formal and informal mentoring relationships. *Journal of Applied Psychology*, 85(4): 529–50.

Ragins, B, Cotton, J and Miller, J (2000) Marginal mentoring: the effects of type of mentor, quality of relationship, and program design on work and career attitudes. *Academy of Management Journal*, 43(6): 1177–94.

Scandura, T (1998) Dysfunctional mentoring relationships and outcomes. *Journal of Management*, 24(3): 449–67.

Wallace, S and Gravells, J (2007a) *Leadership and leading teams*. Exeter: Learning Matters.

Wallace, S and Gravells, J (2007b) *Mentoring* (2nd edn). Exeter: Learning Matters.

Professional skills for reading and writing

This section aims to support and extend your understanding of the text, and to highlight some of the conventions of formal academic writing. It looks at:

- academic vocabulary;
- synthesising information.

It is designed to build your own confidence and skills as both a reader and writer of formal professional or academic texts.

1 Academic vocabulary

Look back over any of the unfamiliar words or phrases that you noted down when reading this chapter. How would you 'translate' these into non-academic language? Here are some specific examples that we pulled out:

- tacit knowledge (page 91);
- observational learning (page 92);
- the prevailing paradigm (page 93);
- contingent characteristics (page 93);
- iterative approach (page 99);
- maintaining ambiguity (page 100).

What is your understanding of the following phrases, used in the context they are here?

- fostering elitism (page 92);
- the widely accepted orthodoxy that successful outcomes in learning relationships are positively correlated with clear and specific goals early on (page 99)?

2 Summarising and synthesising information

There are many examples in this book of the author directly quoting other commentators. However, an alternative to this is to summarise past research, rather than directly quoting from it. For example, how do we know that the list of Hobson et al's (2009) conclusions on pages 91 and 92 are a summary that the writer has made and not a direct quote? The answer is that we know this because a convention requires that a page number be quoted in the reference where a direct quote is made.

One step further is to combine a number of sources and re-present the information in a different way to emphasise particular learning points. There are several examples of this in this chapter, for example in the tables on pages 95 and 97.

You may find it useful to think about how you would synthesise the research on benefits and potential dangers of mentoring, as discussed in this paper, in some sort of table or diagram. Using the information in this chapter, could you link different benefits/dangers to the choices organisations make about how mentoring is used?

Discussion

The discussion topics which follow will help you to explore the relevance of what you have read here to your own experiences and practice, and to support the development of reflection and critical analysis.

DISCUSSION TASK

Look again at the table summarising characteristics of two different views of the mentor's role on page 95. Where does your own institution's approach to mentoring sit relative to these contrasting schools of thought, and is it where they might claim? Does your school or college really want to promote individuality, challenging of the status quo and innovation, or simply to instruct new teachers in how to meet the universal competencies and standards required?

DISCUSSION TASK

Look at the table summarising how different conditions for mentoring may affect outcomes on page 97. Do these suggestions square with your own experience of mentoring and the different conditions under which it can take place? What has characterised the most effective mentoring experiences for you? How does your current experience of mentoring, either as mentor or mentee, correspond to the conditions outlined in this table, and can you recognise any of the positive or negative consequences?

FURTHER READING FURTHER READING **FURTHER READING** FURTHER READING

Of the texts listed above, you may find the following most useful for further reference:

Daloz, L. A. (1999) *Mentor: guiding the journey of adult learners*. San Francisco: Jossey-Bass.

Hobson, A, Ashby, P, Malderez, A and Tomlinson, P (2009) Mentoring beginning teachers: what we know and what we don't. *Teaching and Teacher Education*, 25: 207–16.

Wallace, S and Gravells, J (2007a) *Leadership and leading teams.* Exeter: Learning Matters.

Wallace, S and Gravells, J (2007b) *Mentoring* (2nd edn). Exeter: Learning Matters.

When reading some of the additional texts suggested here, keep an eye out for words and phrases that may be unfamiliar, try to find out what they mean, and think about the context in which they are used. How do the authors combine and synthesise ideas in order to illustrate the points they wish to make? Does this always work successfully, or are there better ways in which the information could have been presented?

10

Institutional issues: the college of further education as a twenty-first century organisation

The aims of this chapter are to provide:

- an introduction to the key features of a college of FE in the twenty-first century;
- a context for study about FE colleges;
- an overview of the political and institutional factors associated with FE and how they may impact on students, staff and the community;
- an examination of the political and policy environment in which FE operates;
- a basis of discussion and development of academic skills;
- suggested additional activity and reading to guide future study.

What to look for

As you read you may find it helpful to consider the following questions.

- How does the interaction in the classroom contribute to quality assurance evaluations?
- How are patterns of working in colleges changing in response to government, awarding body or regulatory demands?
- What agencies are there which can assist the college in achieving its objectives?

Author details

Dr Gill Scott worked in FE colleges as a lecturer, curriculum manager, quality manager, staff development manager and Assistant Principal before moving into HE. Her work in HE has involved teaching on initial teacher training programmes and CPD for staff in colleges and researching into employment practices and policy developments in FE. Gill is currently Dean of the School of Education at Nottingham Trent University and maintains her links with FE through the network of college partners working with the University.

Institutional issues: the college of further education as a twenty-first century organisation

Gill Scott

Abstract

This paper explains the policies and economic factors which have shaped the LLS sector over the past decade. It sets out the way in which FE colleges have developed as a result of these external forces, and looks to the future to identify policy trends which are likely to shape the role and function of colleges, and the working lives of the FE teachers within them.

Introduction

The FE sector is a diverse and changing sector, responding to diverse communities, and most importantly of all, to policy drivers which shape provision and participation.

The sector is subject to a huge amount of political influence in terms of policy requirements, funding changes, initiatives and curriculum changes imposed. At the heart of these policy directives are the economic imperatives that exercise the government. In the main it is international competitiveness and the skills agenda that has exercised them in the last twenty years. More recently the rising unemployment rates linked to economic crisis have shone the spotlight more keenly on the sector as government looks to FE to train young people, retrain unemployed people and work closely with employers to aid their competitiveness. Once again policy decisions on numbers and funding in FE are being amended, as projections regarding the number of places needed in the learning and skills sector are adjusted in response to more demand from 16–19-year-olds faced with poor job prospects and older learners faced with redundancy.

The key to understanding the pressures and changes within the sector is an understanding of the economic and resulting political pressures placed on colleges by national, regional and local politics. Providers are at the mercy of politicians and many of the changes which may seem unco-ordinated within institutions are a result of political policy and pressure. The Learning and Skills Network (LSN) (2009) highlights the lack of connectivity between government departments when it comes to policy for the development of learning and skills, with no consistency between different initiatives or requirements.

The impact of policy on the shape of further education

There has been a plethora of initiatives and reports over the past twenty years, but the current shape of FE and its immediate future have been defined by a number of key political initiatives over the past five years including:

- 14–19 Education and Skills White Paper, 2005;
- Foster Review of FE, 2005;
- Raising Skills, Improving Life Chances White Paper, 2006, and the subsequent Further Education and Training Act 2007;
- World Class Skills, the Leitch Report, 2007.

The Foster review in 2005 stated that FE suffered from many problems, not least lack of coherent and consistent government strategy, with too many bodies having control and influence, too many initiatives, inconsistency in funding decisions and persistent underperformance in some colleges. Central to this, Foster asserts, is a lack of core purpose for the sector. The report concluded that:

> *There is no single, 'magic bullet' solution to FE. Rather through a comprehensive set of reforms across the whole of the FE system, its power to fuel economic achievement through helping individuals realise their personal potential will*

> *provide the basis for a progressive enhancement in FE's standing and esteem in the nation's eyes.*
>
> (Foster, 2005, p3)

Much of the proposed reform and change since then has been in response to this report and its plea for strategic and sweeping reform.

The success of the sector is reflected in the numbers participating in learning, with over a million people benefiting from basic literacy, numeracy and language skills support. In addition the number of young people participating in FE has grown, from 4 million in 1997 to 6 million in 2005. Income to colleges increased by 48 per cent between 1997 and 2006 (DCSF, 2006). But, given the increased participation, this still falls short of the funding levels needed for strategic growth and investment in infrastructure.

Following the Foster Review (2005) the Leitch Report was published in 2007, outlining the skills agenda for the country and setting national targets for training. This report underpins current policy.

As highlighted by the CBI, this report set the stage for major reforms in skills training, with a series of ambitious targets to support international competitiveness by 2020.

> - *Some 95% of adults to have the basic skills of functional literacy and numeracy, up from 85% and 79% respectively in 2005.*
> - *Over 90% of adults qualified to at least Level 2, up from 69% in 2005. A commitment to achieve the review's world-class projection of 95% as soon as possible.*
> - *Shifting the balance of intermediate skills to Level 3. Improving the esteem, quality and quantity of intermediate skills. An additional 1.9 million adults with Level 3 attainments, including boosting the number of apprentices to 500,000 a year.*
> - *Over 40% of adults qualified to Level 4 and above, up from 29% in 2005.*
>
> (CBI, 2009, p6)

Demand-led system is a phrase that is often repeated in government statements. This means that providers are expected to work closely with employers to establish what kinds and levels of skills mix they require now and in the future, and then deliver this mix. The explicit link to economic growth and well-being is clear here: the sector is not to provide learning opportunities for the personal growth of the participant; it is to provide employer-led, demand-led, provision which matches skills to local, regional and national needs.

The aspirations regarding HE within FE have been somewhat muted more recently. The drive to give colleges awarding powers for a new designation of vocational degree has been slowing down, and there is no indication that they will be delivering postgraduate qualifications in any significant numbers. Like all other public sectors, funding for HE has been squeezed recently, and growth in this area is difficult to find. Colleges are in partnership with universities to deliver HE work, and, as universities have had their student numbers capped, funding through that route is unlikely.

In 2007 the government announced the intention to establish twenty new HE centres (within The Further Education and Training Act 2007), assumed to be based on FE college consortia, to widen participation. However, funding changes and more recent investigation of proposals are questioning the viability of these centres and the benefits they may bring. (*THES*, 23.03.09). A small number of centres have recently been announced, but this rapid change of policy and the uncertainty it creates, not only impacts on the future of the sector and the long-term planning model, it also wastes resource, when this is spent on proposals and plans which are subject to changes on political whim. The demand-led approach has been reinforced by government departments:

> *Our goal is a skills and FE system which targets support for individuals and employers where it is needed most, and allows colleges and providers to deliver the excellent service we must have as we move towards a sustainable vision of a high-skills, high-employment, high-productivity nation.*
>
> (DCSF, 2008, p4)

The perceived market for the sector continues to change and develop. In his Foreword to Further Education Colleges – Models for Success, the Secretary of State stated that he wanted the sector to build on its strengths and to go further and:

- *Develop innovative and collaborative learning routes for young people and adults, maximising the opportunities afforded by technology, so that they are truly encouraged and supported to achieve their full potential.*
- *Listen and respond to the needs of employers; building specialised networks that deliver the skills they need, now and in the future.*
- *Reach out to those that are least likely to engage in learning, who lack the skills and confidence they need for success. We want to give these individuals a second chance: give them the opportunity to learn new skills, to move into work and, in doing so, unlock the talent in our communities.*
- *We also want colleges to be recognised for the valuable role they play within their local communities, offering a wide range of opportunities and resources from which local people and businesses benefit.*

> (DIUS, 2008a, p4)

The economic imperative is clear in this statement: meet employer needs and ensure that everyone who can be is economically active. Accompanying this, a very clear policy steer was given in 2008 in the update:

> *We want every 16- and 17-year-old to participate in education or training, and we want every adult to have the chance to improve their skills in order to find work or progress in their current employment. The changing nature of the world economy makes increasing participation in education and training an urgent necessity.*
>
> (DIUS, 2008b, p1)

In effect, this announcement heralded the rise of the school leaving age to 18, in that it expects all people to be in employment, education or training until they are 18. This in itself is a major policy shift, away from encouragement of engagement towards compulsion, in response to the growing number of those not in employment, education or training (NEETs). In the second quarter of 2009 these figures were reported as being 233,000 16–18-year-olds in this category, a rise of 5 per cent on the previous year, and 835,000 18–24-year-olds, a rise of 12 per cent (*TES*b, 21.08.09).

At the same time as increasing the compulsory education or training age, this report also confirmed the place of colleges in delivering the 14–16 vocational education and training agenda, effectively reducing the traditional age at which colleges work with learners. This provision is expected to be delivered in partnership between schools and colleges, a mechanism which should be facilitated by the changes to funding which will bring the funding for learners up to the age of 19 within the remit of the local authority, rather then having different funding bodies (and funding levels) as has been the case since 1992. Control of provision is not being completely devolved to local authorities, however, and it could be seen as being removed further from colleges. Local authorities are expected to create associations to commission activity, rather than working individually with colleges, and in case this is not sufficient to guarantee achievement of the policy agenda:

> This will be supplemented by a national Young People's Learning Agency, which will have reserve powers to step in to secure coherence of plans and budgetary control in the event that agreement cannot be reached.

> (DIUS, 2008b, p9)

The autonomy of colleges, which was a central part of the legislation which created the college corporations, may therefore be seen as being further eroded by central government. In addition, the extension of the role of the college within the community, and the expectations placed upon it to be an engine of change and economic regeneration, may be beyond the scope and resource of many colleges, as reported by the Learning and Skills Improvement Service (LSIS).

> FE College Principals, their senior management teams and FE governors report that they are being stretched beyond their core learning and skills role. This core role itself is characterised by heightened strategic and operational complexities – but is now combined with an ever-widening remit that is encompassing localised economic development and regeneration in its broadest sense.

> (LSIS, 2009, p2)

A further raft of legislation, which formalises the raising of the participation age, will have continuing impact on the sector with the implementation of the Apprenticeship, Skills and Children's Learning Bill, in Spring 2010. This Bill will give local authorities the authority and powers to fulfil their strategic responsibilities associated with raising the participation in education age to 18 by 2015. In order to deliver this the government will create a single point of responsibility and accountability for children's and young people's services from ages 0 to 19, with the aim of having a more co-ordinated provision for young people It will also introduce a new funding system aimed at being responsive to the choices of learners and employers and designed to remove the complex contractual arrangements and bureaucracy that constrain college and employer relationships. In this way the demand-led, employer-linked provision is again stressed, linked to the achievement of the Leitch 2020 targets.

In addition to changing the funding regime for learners under 19, the Apprenticeship, Skills and Children's Learning Bill will also create a new Skills Funding Agency which will take on responsibility for all other learners over the age of 19. It will also, through the National Apprenticeships Service be responsible for securing apprenticeships for 16–18-year-olds and all adults. The Skills Funding Agency will operate through a new demand-led system designed to respond to learner needs. It will be an agency of the Department for Business,

Innovation and Skills (BIS), and will manage a budget of approximately £4 billion (DCSF, 2009a).

The college as a community

As well as directly influencing the activity and finances of colleges, government also attempts to influence the way that provision is delivered and the management of resources, as in this statement on delivery models and employment practices from the Department for Innovation, Universities and Skills (DIUS):

> *Customer-centred delivery models will require colleges to reassess what they are doing and how. This may mean that alternative delivery models are required and that different approaches are needed to meet the needs of different audiences even within one institution. It may require different approaches to managing the college workforce and the use of its physical assets as well as the management of finances.*

> (DIUS, 2008b, p10)

This is an overt statement that employment practice and use of other resource is a matter government departments feel they have a stake in. Although staff contracts, pay, terms and conditions are not within a national framework, political influence is brought to bear on staff issues, especially through the requirements for qualifications and certification within the sector. These requirements and regulations generate change in themselves that may be beyond the control of the college. All teaching staff in the sector are now required to achieve qualifications endorsed by Skills Verification UK (SVUK), based on national standards for teaching qualifications. This has created the status of QTLS, in an attempt to give parity with the Qualified Teacher Status (QTS) of school teachers. However, the salary gap and the lack of transferability between the two sectors leads many to conclude that equal status remains a long way off. The changing nature of the client group and the role of lecturers, especially when working with employers, has led to the development of many new teaching and learning roles in colleges. These roles are based more on those found in industry-linked training organisations, where staff assess and monitor progress, working with trainees on a one-to-one basis to plug skill and knowledge gaps, rather than teaching. This has led to the development of assessor, trainer and verifier roles, often on support staff contracts rather than academic ones, and a further change in the status and rewards of teaching and learning staff in colleges (Scott, 2005).

The changing nature of learners has an impact on the work undertaken by the staff within the institution. Jephcote et al (2008) report that teaching staff in colleges document a large part of their role as dealing with the personal issues which learners bring with them. This may increase as the number of under-16s and NEETs in colleges increases. According to Jephcote, despite all the policy and bureaucracy, lecturers see the interaction with the learners, and helping learners to succeed, as the central part of their role. This may at times mean cutting corners to ensure that records are kept and students have a supportive experience, possibly at the expense of engaging and innovating learning activities. If learners present with such major personal problems that they are prevented from engaging meaningfully with learning, then the lecturer's first role is to help them with the personal issues; but what does this mean for the role of the lecturer, and for the targets they have to meet? Jephcote's research showed that:

> *Commonly, teachers privileged what they perceived to be the needs and interests of learners, which might or might not have coincided with the demands being placed on them by college managers. Without exception, pedagogical expertise, which in large part was about forging supportive relationships with students, was considered more important than expertise in subject matter. As they viewed it, 'success' was based on establishing appropriate relationships, and building these relationships was a vital component of changing learners' behaviours.*
>
> (Jephcote et al, 2008, p170)

FE has long been seen as the sector which meets employer needs for vocational and professional training, and the political direction of policy at the moment is heightening that emphasis, with government attempting to respond to economic pressure that may have an impact for many years to come (LSN, 2009). Employer groups as well as government are seeking to influence policy and practice through reports on vocational education and training, as the CBI states:

> *Further education colleges are well-established as a major source of training provision. Many already have strong links with employers. The government is committed to supporting colleges to work more effectively with businesses in the coming years, putting learners and employers in the driving seat to reinforce a demand-led approach.*
>
> (CBI, 2009, p4)

The key point here is the *demand-led approach* identified by the CBI. This implies demand from employers, not learners, with the economic imperative the main driver behind the design and delivery of training. For colleges to effectively engage with employers and contribute to the skills and economic development of their local and regional community they are encouraged to design programmes to meet employer needs, rather than those of learners. The CBI encourages colleges to make a commitment to employer engagement throughout a college, through the following:

- *A focus on the employer as primary client*
- *Getting the message across to employers of what colleges have to offer*
- *Conducting dialogue about training in business terms*
- *Having a clear and responsive college point of contact for employers*
- *The value of effective CRM [Central Resource Management] systems*
- *The benefits of explicit service standards*
- *Drawing on the college USPs [Unique Selling Points] of continuity and funding expertise*
- *Having the right staff in place to deliver employer-backed programmes*
- *Achieving flexibility in delivery*
- *Building networks with other training providers*
- *Motivating the learners*
- *Managing funding effectively*
- *Agreeing measurable objectives for each programme*
- *Drawing on the experience of work with employers to enhance college effectiveness.*

(CBI, 2009, p13)

How this agenda of employer engagement can be reconciled with the focus on personalised learning and support for learners, who have often had a poor educational experience in the past, is a question that continues to tax colleges and delivery teams. Flexibility is seen as key to meeting the skills and economic agenda. Providing a range of progression routes through established training routes is recognised as the most effective way of creating successful programmes (LSN, 2009). In this way it may be possible to bring together employer and learner needs and government policy and funding drivers. As part of this agenda of flexibility and employer engagement, colleges are encouraged to enter into partnerships with employers, schools and private training organisations. However these are not without their costs and pitfalls, as Giwa notes:

> The current 'top down' approach used by funding agencies such as the LSC, characterised by funding levers, which compel providers to form partnerships can be problematic... I also found that the huge opportunity costs, in terms of management and administrative costs, for setting up such enforced partnerships can sometimes outweigh the perceived benefits of using collaborative practices to widen participation.
>
> (2008, p101)

Partnership is central to the government's agenda for delivery of both the children's agenda and economic well-being and growth for the community. Colleges are increasingly being expected to work in partnership. In a time of declining numbers of 18–20-year-olds, key elements of colleges' core market may be the subject of increasing competition, requiring colleges to work in partnership for delivery of vocational subjects with schools, local authorities and employers/private trainers. A collaborative delivery model for the 14–19 provision, including NVQs and Diplomas, is the most likely scenario when funding is controlled through local authorities and numbers of learners in the system are declining. Giwa comments on this approach:

> Collaborative approaches have become increasingly prevalent in the delivery of post-compulsory education and training and have been seen by the government as a means of moving beyond the marketised approaches (where colleges compete to sell their products to consumers) to delivery of post-compulsory education and training,
>
> (Giwa, 2008, p80)

This type of collaboration may therefore bring benefits and remove the competitive drive that has been imposed on colleges since 1992. However, the divide between the expectations of 14–19 education and training, possibly through a collaborative model, and the demand-led post-19 model linked to employer needs, leaves little room for colleges to establish their unique selling points and the added value proposition they can deliver for learners.

Demographics

As the demographic pattern of the population changes, so do the pressures placed on colleges and the market that they are addressing. As the CBI notes, colleges are increasingly seen as catering for the work-based and workforce training market, rather than the 14–19 market, which may become the province of schools entirely, or have colleges as junior partners.

The policy push for FE colleges to become more active in workforce development coincides with a significant demographic shift. In the years ahead, the age group of young people who have traditionally formed the mainstay of the college population will shrink. In the decade after 2010–11 the number of 18–20 year-olds will decline by more than 12%. If colleges are to maintain and/or grow their volume of teaching activity, they will have to reach out on a larger scale to other age groups and to those already at work.

(CBI, 2009, p6)

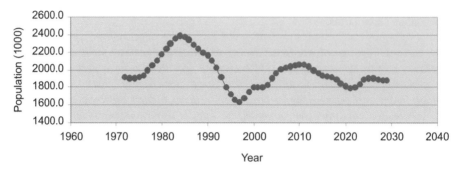

Year

Figure 10.1 18–20 population projections 1972–2030 (DfES from ONS population estimates and GAD projections)

As shown in Figure 10.1, the number of 18–20-year-olds hits its peak in 2010, which means that the number of 16–19-year-olds has already peaked and will now decline over the next 20 years. The birth rate has been increasing since 2005, and this will start to have an impact on colleges in 2016, as demonstrated on the graph; but the numbers will still remain well below the 1985 and 2010 peaks. The market for colleges will therefore change as more people are in the workforce, probably for longer as changes to the retirement age also begin to have an impact, and fewer people are in the 14–25 age range accessing initial education and training progression from school. The impact of these changes on the market and provision of colleges is still unclear, especially when the additional consideration of economic turmoil is factored in.

Funding

Funding rules and bodies change, and below is an outline of the latest legislation. But the significance is not in the detail of the changes, which managers need to keep on top of; the important consideration is that it is a very political environment and it is vital that managers understand the political drivers behind the changes, so that they are able to anticipate the policy direction.

Alongside the demographic changes, the government has instituted funding and legislative changes which will create a divide between under-19 education and training, and that for the over-19s. This split between under-19 and over-19 indicates government intention to:

- raise the compulsory education age to 18;
- integrate children's services;
- facilitate local and regional priorities and agendas;
- facilitate employer engagement and influence on training.

Subject to the approval of the Apprenticeships, Skills, Children and Learning (ASCL) Bill, the funding for education for people up to the age of 18 (including those in colleges and sixth form colleges) will pass to the local authority, and away from the separate LSC. This is a partial reversion to the funding arrangements prior to the 1989 Education Reform Act which gave colleges single line budgets from the LEA and led subsequently to 'Incorporation' in 1992 which separated control and funding of FE and sixth form colleges from LEAs and gave colleges the status of corporate bodies.

Education for the over-18s will transfer to the new Skills Funding Agency at the same time as the LSC is disbanded. This will mean that colleges will be working with at least two different agencies for funding the same provision where there are under-18s and over-18s in the same classrooms. Obvious bureaucratic issues are raised here. For example: Will the funding levels be the same? Will reporting and outcome requirements be the same? Or will dual systems be forced to operate? Questions about students who cross local authority boundaries will also arise. Will it be the authority in which the college is based who is responsible for the funding, or the authority where the student is based? According to the DCSF:

> *Local authorities will come together as a regional planning group in each of the nine Government Office regions to consider and agree the overall commissioning plan for the region. The Regional Development Agency (RDA) will co-chair this group, which will be convened by the Young People's Learning Agency and include representatives from the Government Office and the adult Skills Funding Agency.*
>
> (DCSF, 2008b, p6)

A further aim of the ASCL Bill 2009 is to radically overhaul apprenticeships, bringing apprentice training back up the agenda alongside the development of vocational diplomas, and setting work-based training up as an option alongside academic work. The DCSF says:

> *The Apprenticeships, Skills, Children and Learning Bill provides the first complete overhaul of Apprenticeships legislation for nearly 200 years. The new legislation will put apprenticeships on a statutory basis, establish the entitlement to an apprenticeship place for every suitably qualified young person who wants one and will ensure a good quality apprenticeship for apprentices and employers alike. It will help to meet Ministers' ambitions that one in five young people will undertake an apprenticeship by 2020,*
>
> (2009b)

Whether the apprenticeship training will be done in colleges or through employers and private training organisations is still to be seen. Previous government skills training routes for young people have relied heavily on private training organisations to facilitate employment and work-based training, with colleges sometimes providing off the job training or assessment.

The Skills Funding Agency will have the remit of drawing together the different agencies concerned with training for the over-19s. According to the DIUS:

> *The key role of the new Skills Funding Agency is to ensure that public money is routed swiftly, efficiently and securely to FE Colleges and providers following the purchasing decisions of customers.*
>
> (2008b, p9)

This agency will administer Train to Gain and Skills Accounts to ensure that the system is demand led. The agency will have a direct influence on provision.

> *This includes responding to strategic skills pressures and bottlenecks, securing dynamic market exit and entry, creating a funding and incentive structure that prioritises responsiveness to customers, and ensuring availability of good public information.*

> (Ibid)

It is claimed that the Skills Funding Agency will be a funding body, not a funding and planning body, but it is difficult to see how the above objective can be achieved without some influence on planning at an institutional level. The major thrust will be to ensure that providers create provision aimed at up-skilling the workforce to meet the nation's needs, the economic imperative writ large. In addition, and noted below, this agency will be responsible for the performance management of colleges and have the power of intervention if colleges do not meet standards. The full implications of these powers will remain to be seen.

This is a wide remit which will also necessitate an interface with local authorities and employers as well as links to school funding and qualification policy. The funding arrangements for colleges have been subject to repeated change since 1989, often at very short notice. There is little doubt that such a politically sensitive area as skills training and education will continue to be subject to intervention and funding change.

Quality assurance

OFSTED conduct inspections of colleges and rate their performance, including how well the college self assesses its own quality assurance and performance. They report that:

> *The further education college sector is improving. Inspection grades over time demonstrate a trajectory of improvement: just over 60% of colleges are now categorised as good or better compared to just under 50% at the end of the 2001–05 cycle. Overall success rates in 2006/07 were 77.7%, compared to 60% in 2000/01. There is a low incidence of college inadequacy which is now close to 4%.*

> (OFSTED, 2008, p4)

As this is the published account of the quality of provision in colleges, it is important that colleges are seen to be implementing what OFSTED regard as best practice and developing their provision, systems and support mechanisms in line with their expectations. In 2008 OFSTED conducted a desk survey, followed up with some focused visits to providers to identify what key factors help colleges to improve. They acknowledge that the background and context of the college will have a major impact on the operation, culture and portfolio of the college, and that there is no one best model. However, they do assert that there are some features which characterise capacity for quality improvement (OFSTED, 2008). Governors and managers are charged by OFSTED with assessing whether their college matches the features of an effective college. These include, under the heading of 'Overall effectiveness', the need to:

- *Clarify the mission and the vision and the values required for delivery. Make sure they are understood by staff and key stakeholders.*
- *Involve the staff in shaping strategies to deliver the mission. Deal with their apprehensions, respond to their concerns and empower them to contribute.*

- *Communicate and listen. Share all information with staff and keep no hidden agendas.*
- *Make sure the resources, including staff, match the delivery of the mission. If not, retrain or reconfigure.*
- *Be impatient for success. Do the hard things first and make the impatience infectious.*
- *Build trust, be visible – live the vision and values with integrity.*
- *Set high expectations and invite staff to do the same for themselves and their students. Make 'satisfactory is not good enough' your and their mantra.*
- *Celebrate success – of individuals, teams and the institution as a whole.*

(OFSTED, 2008, p30)

And, under the heading of 'Achievement and standards' the need to:

- *Encourage teams to pursue excellence and eliminate any tendency to aspire to be average by simply focusing on eliminating weaknesses.*
- *Get the data right and make sure governors, managers and staff can interpret them.*
- *Review, revisit and review again. Keep systems smart and slim. Reduce unnecessary administrative procedures. Involve staff and middle managers in leading system reviews.*
- *Target and prioritise. Identify key barriers and drill down to investigate the issues.*

(Ibid)

Under the heading, 'Quality of provision' they are required to:

- *Get the curriculum offer right to match the needs of your students.*
- *Get the advice right at entry. Make sure parents, potential students and employers are well informed. Give students options to succeed, not just options to study.*
- *Make sure you thoroughly analyse the individual needs of students, not just at entry but throughout their course. Broaden your definition of students at risk; target them with support and monitor their progress closely.*
- *Encourage innovation. Regard compliance as a necessary but not sufficient goal of success. Make sure that systems contribute to success and do not demand compliance for their own sake. At the same time encourage innovation and initiative.*
- *Build a culture of critical self-review. Make sure quality assurance is also quality improvement. Make self-assessment, action planning, support and target-setting a seamless process. Avoid diagnosis without prescription.*
- *Focus on improving the students' experience in the round. Do not focus exclusively on teaching and learning. Review curriculum structure and delivery. Make sure students can enjoy as well as achieve.*

(Ibid)

And in terms of 'Leadership and management' colleges must demonstrate that they can:

- *Build informed governance. Tackle underperforming governance. Train governors to be challenging, not just supportive, and to play their part in an informed way in shaping the mission.*
- *Train and retrain your middle managers, as individuals and as a team.*

> *Empower them to drive the mission and to have confidence in their roles.*
>
> (Ibid)

During inspections OFSTED will assess how close colleges are to this model of best practice and their capacity to improve, based on action plans, self-evaluation and awareness of development issues.

Under the Further Education and Training Act the Skills Funding Agency will be established to fund provision for learners over the age of 19. In addition it will have a quality and monitoring role for all provision in colleges, adding another inspection layer:

> *...The Skills Funding Agency will therefore be responsible for the performance management of FE Colleges. It will also be the single point of intervention where either pre- or post-19 performance of FE Colleges does not meet nationally agreed minimum standards.*
>
> (DIUS 2008a, p11)

In this way it is likely that OFSTED will provide the evidence of quality assurance, quality enhancement and impact of provision, on which the Skills Funding Agency will act if it is below the expected levels of performance.

Governance and management

It is acknowledged in the report by the Leaning and Skills Improvement Agency (Gibney et al, 2009) that FE is one of the most regulated public sectors in the UK, with 2.6 per cent of its budget being spent on regulatory matters and processes. It is possible that the heavy regulation has caused lack of flexibility and responsiveness in the sector, as college management teams become risk averse. The government indicated in 2006 that it wanted the sector (along with other public sector bodies) to be more self regulating. This was reinforced in 2009 by the Prime Minister, Gordon Brown:

> *We know that real excellence depends upon liberating the imagination, creativity and commitment of the public service workforce. This requires us to create new opportunities for professionals to take control of the process of change – with less top-down control and a greater say for front-line staff.*
>
> (Brown, 2009, p4)

And:

> *Government... must step up its efforts to cut unnecessary targets, strip out waste, and devolve responsibility to communities, councils and local service providers.*
>
> (Ibid)

However, the perceived failure of self-regulation in the financial sector in recent years has changed the emphasis and reduced government enthusiasm for self-regulation. As stated above, the new Skills Training Agency will have an additional intervention role, on top of those quality and audit checks already in place, and that will be to address perceived under-performance against targets.

Governors play a key role in setting the strategic direction, tone and ethos of the college. They represent the local community, and part of their role is to ensure financial stability, maintain standards and monitor the contribution the college makes to that community. They set the evaluation framework within which the college management implements strategy and operates day to day. OFSTED recognises the centrality of governors, arguing that effective governors:

> recognise that [they] need to supply high level, constructive challenges, not only in relation to strategic direction and mission, but aimed at assuring achievements and standards, and the quality of provision.

> (OFSTED, 2008, p20)

The Further Education and Training Act 2007 enacts key aspects of the FE reforms described in the March 2006 White Paper, Further Education: Raising Skills, Improving Life Chances. The intention is that the FE system will be able to increase participation and achievement still further and so play its full part in achieving the skills challenge articulated by Lord Leitch. This extends the remit of colleges, and the responsibilities of governors and managers.

The Act includes:

- powers which will enable the specification of FE institutions in England to award their own foundation degrees;
- provision enabling the LSC, in certain circumstances specified in the Act, to intervene in the management of unsatisfactory FE provision in England, with similar powers for Welsh Ministers to intervene in institutions in Wales;
- new requirements on the LSC and on FE institutions to have regard to guidance in relation to consultation with learners, potential learners and employers;
- provision for a restructuring of and new duties on the LSC to make it more responsive to the changing requirements of employers and learners;
- provision enabling the Secretary of State to specify bodies to act as strategy-making bodies in relation to the exercise of the LSC's functions in a particular area;
- provision enabling the Secretary of State to require all principals to achieve a leadership qualification;
- measures which will facilitate the use of new and innovative delivery models, such as trusts and mergers;
- detailed changes to the arrangements for demonstrating employer support for proposals for industrial training levies and to the process for levy orders;
- provision widening the scope for the LSC to deliver shared services;
- an extension of the legislative competence of the National Assembly for Wales in relation to various education and training matters.

This 2007 Act has the potential to have a major impact on the governance of colleges, with a move away from centralised agenda setting towards the community that the college serves, in a way which the Learning and Skills Improvement Service (LSIS) views as desirable,

> College governance does not operate in a vacuum: it involves governors, chairs, principals, professionals, senior managers, clerks, community and wider stake-holders. It also acts as a prism through which complex policy-practice imperatives are mediated at local level.

> (LSIS, 2009, p2)

As colleges are increasingly being seen as community partners, rather than the controllers of resource and knowledge, their emphasis is expected to move towards links with the community and services which meet the needs of that community. The community has broad boundaries, and not all members will have the same desires, demands or expectations of the college, which is why the governors need to set the tone for the college which is inclusive and welcoming. Employers, schools, parents, young people, adult learners, local authorities, children's services and residents are among those who make up the college community, and the college has to respond in a creative way to their needs. This does not mean that they necessarily will be able to meet every one of these needs, but it does require that governors and senior managers should take time to reflect on the ethos and purpose of the college and how it relates to and inter-relates with its community.

The relationship between governors and managers in the college is crucial to the success of the enterprise, and particularly the relationship between the Chair of governors and the Principal. This professional relationship has to be supportive but challenging, informed but impartial and regular without being overwhelming. Governors approve strategy, finances and curriculum; they then step back and monitor how well the managers deliver the strategy. This important relationship and definition of roles is embodied within The Instruments and Articles of Governance (DIUS, 2002d), the rules by which governors operate. These outline the responsibilities of governors as:

(a) *the determination and periodic review of the educational character and mission of the institution and the oversight of its activities;*
(b) *approving the quality strategy of the institution;*
(c) *the effective and efficient use of resources, the solvency of the institution and the Corporation and safeguarding their assets;*
(d) *approving annual estimates of income and expenditure;*
(e) *the appointment, grading, suspension, dismissal and determination of the pay and conditions of service of the holders of senior posts and the Clerk, including, where the Clerk is, or is to be appointed as, a member of staff, the Clerk's appointment, grading, suspension, dismissal and determination of pay in the capacity of a member of staff; and*
(f) *setting a framework for the pay and conditions of service of all other staff.*

(DIUS, 2007, p13)

Changes were made to these articles in 2009 to reflect the changes in the Further Education and Training Act 2007 removing control from the LSC. The role that the government sees for colleges led by governors is a central one within the community.

The three key players – community, business and learners – are again aligned here, as central to delivering the economic agenda of the government and the future competitiveness of the local and national economy. The central role, and the level of expectations placed upon governors by regulatory and inspection bodies, led to a report by the LSIS in 2009 which claimed that:

Despite the fast changing period of transition and diverse contexts in which colleges operate... Governance works best when governors, managers and clerks participate in shared activities through training days, workshops and strategy groups/committees. Much good governance practice takes place beyond desig-nated board meetings and often goes unrecognised. Managers and governors need to build on such non formal learning cultures.

(LSIS, 2009a, p3)

Such informal learning and sharing activities may be seen as beneficial in generating creative governance, but is it in the best spirit of the OFSTED requirement quoted above, where the distance between governors and managers is vital to the accountability and monitoring function? The LSIS report makes recommendations for effective and creative governance, including improved training, placing learning and teaching at the heart of their considera-tions and a model of reflexive, rather than reactive governance. The creativity of governance is seen, by LSIS, to be currently restricted by the audit culture and changing funding regimes (LSIS, 2009).

Despite the huge agenda which FE is being expected to deliver and the continuous change imposed by government and government agencies, there is some optimism on the part of college managers, and a feeling that the emphasis on learning and skills can only be a good thing for colleges. This emphasis may remove the Cinderella sector tag at last, as the real contribution that colleges make to their local, regional and national community is recog-nised, alongside the impact they have on the lives of individuals.

Conclusion

Colleges continue to face challenges in the twenty-first century, and will continue to rise to them. Each teacher – indeed, the whole college community – needs to be aware of the environment and climate within which they operate, not only locally but also regionally and nationally. Political pressures will continue to be exerted, and colleges will be expected to respond quickly and effectively. As we have seen, there has been a range of policy initiatives in the last decade alone, some of which appear to have not been carried through, and others, such as degree awarding powers, which seem to have been quietly dropped. It is the core mission of FE, that of providing vocational and lifelong training opportunities to meet the need of employers, which is currently back to the top of the list of priorities, and funding is currently being directed at that aspect rather than others. It is therefore imperative that college governors and managers continue to operate mechanisms for scanning their environment for opportunities and potential threats, so that they can respond quickly and appropriately, and influence the local and national skills and training agenda as well as being shaped by it.

References

Brown, G (2009) Foreword to *Excellence and fairness: achieving world class public services*. London: Cabinet Office.

CBI (2009) *Reaching further: workforce development through employer – FE college partnership*. London: CBI.

Denham, J (2007) *Secretary of State, John Denham's speech to the Association of Colleges conference*. 22 November 2007.

Department for Children, Schools and Families (2006) Further education White Paper: transforming young lives and driving up skills for the future. Press release 27 March 2006, Press Notice 2006/0045. Available: **www.dcsf.gov.uk/pns/DisplayPN.cgi?pn_id=2006_0045** (accessed November 2009).

Department for Children, Schools and Families (2008a) Post-16 reforms factsheet. Available: **publications.dcsf.gov.uk/eOrderingDownload/Post-16-Reforms-Factsheet.doc** (accessed November 2009).

Department for Children, Schools and Families (2008b) *Raising expectations: enabling the system to deliver*. London: DCSF.

Department for Children, Schools and Families (2009a) *Apprenticeships, Skills, Children and Learning Bill*. London: DCSF.

Department for Children, Schools and Families (2009b) *New Bill to equip the country in meeting the education and skills needs of the economy*. Press release 5 February 2009. Available: **www.dcsf.gov.uk/pns/DisplayPN.cgi?pn_id=2009_0025** (accessed November 2009).

Department for Innovation, Universities and Skills (2007a) *Further education: raising skills, improving life changes*. London: DIUS.

Department for Innovation, Universities and Skills (2007b) *Further education: raising skills, improving life changes: an update.* London: DIUS.

Department for Innovation, Universities and Skills (2007c) Further Education and Training Act press release October 2007 Raising skills, improving life chances.

Department for Innovation, Universities and Skills (2007d) Instrument and Articles of Governance. London: DIUS.

Department for Innovation, Universities and Skills (2008a) Further education colleges – models for success. London: DIUS. **Available: www.dius.gov.uk/further_education/fe_reform/skills-funding-agency-transition/~/media/publications/R/RasingExpectationsSummarydocument** (accessed November 2009).

Department for Innovation, Universities and Skills (2008b) Raising expectations: enabling the system to deliver. London: DIUS.

Foster A (2005) *Realising the potential. A review of the future role of further education colleges.* Annesley: DfES Publications.

Gibney, J, Yapp, C, Trickett, L and Collinge, C (2009) *The 'new' place-shaping: the implications for leaders in the further education sector.* LSIS Research Programme 2008–9.

Giwa, M (2008) How effective are collaborative approaches for widening participation in further education and training? *Research in Post-Compulsory Education,* 13(1): 79–105.

Jephcote, M, Salisbury, J and Rees, G (2008) Being a teacher in further education in changing times. *Research in Post-Compulsory Education*, 13(2): 163–172.

LSIS (2009) *Creative governance in further education: the art of the possible?* London: LSIS.

LSN (2009) Beyond Leitch: skills policy for the upturn – how skills can rebuild the economy. Available: **www.lsnlearning.org.uk** (accessed November 2009).

OFSTED (2008) How colleges improve. Available: **www.ofsted.gov.uk** (accessed November 2009).

Scott, G (2005) Para-professionals in further education: changing roles in vocational delivery. *Management in Education*, 19(4): 24–27.

Professional skills for reading and writing

This section aims to support and extend your understanding of the text, and to highlight some of the conventions of formal academic or professional writing. It looks at the use of charts and graphs to summarise or clarify numerical information; the various wordings which can be used to introduce quoted material; and the use of figurative language and 'shorthand'.

1 Charts and graphs

This paper makes use of a graph showing clearly how the numbers of potential students in a particular age group peak during certain years. You will have noticed that this graph is clearly labelled. We can see at a glance that one axis represents years and the other represents the numbers in that age group. You will also no doubt have noticed that the author follows the graph with a discussion of what it illustrates and the significance of the information it conveys. The learning point here is that it is always important, when using graphs or charts, that they should be a) clearly labelled, b) relevant to the subject or argument, and c) preceded or followed by a discussion of what they show.

2 Introducing quoted material

This paper makes extensive use of quotations from government papers and other policy documents. You may find it useful to go back through the paper to see how each quote is introduced. Phrases used include:

- Jephcote's research showed that:
- According to the DCSF:
- These outline the responsibilities of governors as:
- The report concluded that:

It is important, when including quoted material, that the transition from your own writing to the quoted passage should be both grammatical and clear. It is also important not to use the same phrase or word each time. A much over-used word in this context is 'states'. You should try to find various and meaningful ways of linking to quotes, as this writer has done.

Did you notice how the writer referenced quotes from the educational press? The important factor to remember here is that when you are quoting from, or referring to, an article in the press, the year alone will not be accurate enough to identify the source clearly, and so you will need to give the full date, as this author does. For example:

'In the second quarter of 2009 these figures were reported as being 233,000 16–18-year-olds in this category, a rise of 5 per cent on the previous year, and 835,000 18–24-year-olds, a rise of 12 per cent (*TES*, 21.08.09)'

You may also have noticed the use of (Ibid) to identify a reference. This Latin abbreviation is a useful one. It means: This is from exactly the same source (and page number, if relevant) as the previous quote I have just cited.

3 The use of figurative language and 'shorthand'

Every profession has its own familiar figures of speech and 'shorthand'. Sometimes, for example when we are not familiar with this vocabulary, we might refer to it as 'jargon'. Consider the following examples taken from this paper, all of which suggest that it was written for a readership with a specific interest in the LLS. What do you take them to mean?

- *The Cinderella sector tag.*
- *College management teams become risk averse.*
- *Plug skill and knowledge gaps, rather than teaching.*
- *The economic imperative.*
- *Funding for HE has been squeezed recently.*
- *Universities have had their student numbers capped.*

What other examples can you find in this paper?

Discussion

The suggestions for further research and discussion which follow will help you to explore the relevance of what you have read here to your own institution and professional practice.

DISCUSSION TASK

Research the latest OFSTED reports on effective college provision and audit your college against the criteria for success.

DISCUSSION TASK

Research the latest funding methodology and assess if there are ways of increasing the resource allocation through curriculum design or delivery, to the benefit of the learners.

DISCUSSION TASK

- Consider what developments are happening in your area in terms of 14–19 vocational education collaboration, and how this impacts on choice for learners and the management, quality and development of the organisations concerned.
- What local and regional priorities are colleges in your area expected to respond to?

DISCUSSION TASK

Who are the governors in your college, and who do they represent?

FURTHER READING FURTHER READING **FURTHER READING** FURTHER READING

You can follow up your reading of this paper by looking for papers specifically related to policies of current relevance to your college and your practice in journals such as *Research in Post-Compulsory Education*, which is available in hard copy or online. For online access, contact your college librarian.

For example, two papers from this journal listed in the references for this chapter will be of particular interest. They are:

Giwa, M (2008) How effective are collaborative approaches for widening participation in further education and training? *Research in Post-Compulsory Education*, 13:1, 7–105.
Jephcote, M, Salisbury, J and Rees, G (2008) Being a teacher in further education in changing times, *Research in Post-Compulsory Education*, 13:2, 163–172.

You will also find it useful to read Chapter 2 in this book, which examines some of the same legislation mentioned in the chapter, but from the point of view of its impact on you as a teacher, rather than on the college as an institution.

You may also find the following of interest:

Muijs, D, Harris, A, Lumby, J, Morrison, M and Sood, K (2006) Leadership and leadership development in highly effective further education providers. Is there a relationship? *Journal of Further and Higher Education*, 30(1): 87–106.

Appendix 1
Coverage of LLUK Professional Standards for Teachers

Chapter 1: AS4; AS7; BK2.3; BS2; CS2; CS4; DS3; ES4; ES5; FS3
Chapter 2: AS4; AK6.1; AK6.2; CK1.2
Chapter 3: AS4; DK1.1; DK2.1; DK3.1
Chapter 4: AS1; AS2; AS3; AS4; BS1; DS1; FS1
Chapter 5: AS3; AS4; AK1.1; AK3.1; CK3.3; CK3.4; FK1.1
Chapter 6: AS4; EK1.1; EK2.1; EK2.2; EK3.1; EK4.1; EK4.2
Chapter 7: AS4; AP4.3; AK4.3; AS7; DK3.1;
Chapter 8: AS4; AK5.1; BK3.5; BK4.1; DK3.2; FK4.2
Chapter 9: BK2.6; BK2.7; BK3.1; BK3.3; DK3.1; EK1.3
Chapter 10: AS4; AK2.2; AK6.1; CK1.2

Appendix 2
Professional skills for reading and writing

An index of professional skills for reading and writing

Professional skills for reading and writing listed chapter by chapter

Chapter 1: Discussion and guidance on style and tone, and on the use of the first person, 'I', in academic writing.

Chapter 2: Guidance on key aspects of formal academic writing, including abbreviations, acronyms and abstracts.

Chapter 3: Reading and writing research papers: conventions and presentational issues.

Chapter 4: Citing relevant literature correctly; and how quotation and citation can be used effectively in academic writing to support an argument.

Chapter 5: The use of chronologies, reference material, and personal experience; and how these can be presented to support and illustrate academic argument.

Chapter 6: The conventions governing the use of appendices in formal writing.

Chapter 7: The use of section headings and topic sentences.

Chapter 8: Referencing works by more than one author, and referencing websites.

Chapter 9: Synthesising information, and using and understanding the specialised vocabulary relevant to the teacher's role.

Chapter 10: The use of charts and graphs; useful phrases for introducing quotes; how to reference quotes from newspapers; how to use the term 'Ibid'; and how the use of figurative language can enliven a piece of writing.